AN ILLUSTRATED GUIDE TO
TRACING YOUR FAMILY HISTORY

JAMES GIBB

T&J

Our Family Tree

Wife's side (left):

- great great grandfather
- great great grandmother
- great great grandfather
- great great grandmother
- great great grandfather
- great great grandmother
- great great grandfather
- great great grandmother
- great grandfather
- great grandmother
- great grandfather
- great grandmother
- grandfather
- grandmother

- great great grandfather
- great great grandmother
- great great grandfather
- great great grandmother
- great great grandfather
- great great grandmother
- great great grandfather
- great great grandmother
- great grandfather
- great grandmother
- great grandfather
- great grandmother
- grandfather
- grandmother

Husband's side (right):

- great great grandfather
- great great grandmother
- great great grandfather
- great great grandmother
- great great grandfather
- great great grandmother
- great great grandfather
- great great grandmother
- great grandfather
- great grandmother
- great grandfather
- great grandmother
- grandfather
- grandmother

- great great grandfather
- great great grandmother
- great great grandfather
- great great grandmother
- great great grandfather
- great great grandmother
- great great grandfather
- great great grandmother
- great grandfather
- great grandmother
- great grandfather
- great grandmother
- grandfather
- grandmother

Father   **Wife** _(your name)_   Mother

Father   **Husband** _(your name)_   Mother

Wife's Brothers and Sisters
Listed Below:

married to

married to

Children

married to

Children

married to

Children

married to

Children

Husband's Brothers and Sisters
Listed Below:

married to

married to

Children

married to

Children

married to

Children

married to

Children

Wife's Maternal Aunts and Uncles
Listed Below:

married to:
children:

married to:
children:

married to:
children:

married to:
children:

Our Children

married to

children

married to

children

married to

children

married to

children

Husband's Maternal Aunts and Uncles
Listed Below:

married to:
children:

married to:
children:

married to:
children:

Wife's Paternal Aunts and Uncles
Listed Below:

married to

Children

married to

Children

married to

Children

married to

Children

Husband's Paternal Aunts and Uncles
Listed Below:

married to

married to

Children

married to

Children

married to

Children

CONTENTS

INTRODUCTION

The object of this book is to encourage and to assist people who are pursuing the intricate stories which make up the history of their ancestors. This is about much more than just obtaining a collection of names and dates.

Every family has a history which is worth investigating even though some of the occupations and locations of our forebears might be a little mundane. It should not surprise anyone, particularly those with relatives in Great Britain, that in the 19th century most of their predecessors would have been described as agricultural labourers. Similar descriptions would certainly apply to ancestors from other European countries as, until industrialisation, most people who worked were employed in agriculture.

It was only as the 19th century developed that we find jobs connected to the textile, mining and manufacturing industries becoming common. In parallel with these, large numbers were employed as domestic servants, reflecting the new middle and upper classes who were able to afford to employ others.

There were large movements of people in the 19th century as people sought better pay and conditions. The emigration from Europe of substantial numbers to America, Australia, New Zealand, South America and South Africa dispersed families all over the world, with the attendant difficulties of now locating their places of origin and relatives.

It is tempting for many of us to assume that we are descended from a famous historical figure. However, this is rarely the case. It is usually a time consuming and fruitless exercise to trace the descendants of a famous figure, as the researcher's family is rarely included. So the best advice is always to work from the known to the unknown, starting with yourself, then parents, grandparents, leading to more distant relatives.

In pursuing your family history we are going to show you many of the sources of relevant data as well as various

An enigma - who is this child, is it a girl or a boy? On the back there is the date 1895. The other writing on the rear of the photograph is illegible. This is an example of why it is important to identify clearly subjects in photographs. In this period boys were often dressed as girls until they were four or five years of age. This makes the task of identifying the child even more difficult, but it also makes the whole subject of family history a demanding and fascinating pursuit.

methods of obtaining appropriate information in order to attain your goals.

A surprising amount of memorabilia has been unearthed during personal research into my own family history. Copies of many of the relevant documentation are reproduced in this book. They provide signposts to other potential family history researchers. In other words, they indicate the wealth of information which is available

Somerset House in London, UK, was home from 1837 for the registrar general of births, marriages and deaths. These records are now housed at the national archives in Kew.

INTRODUCTION

The National Archives Building, known informally as Archives I, located north of the National Mall on Constitution Avenue in Washington, D.C., opened as its original headquarters in 1935.

in most families. Naturally my personal momentos are of most worth and interest to members of my own extended family. Nevertheless they are used here to stimulate intrigue and eagerness in others so that they experience a keen desire to discover similar data from their own family archives. They will then find that such data constitute the jigsaw pieces which can be fitted together to complete a comprehensive picture of a family's history. My own search for information about my ancestors has proved to be a fascinating, all-consuming hobby. It has revealed information of which I had no previous knowledge. Above all, it has necessitated contact with long forgotten friends and family and the building of new fulfilling relationships.

The National Archives at Kew, UK..

CHAPTER 1: GETTING STARTED

Starting any project, such as exploring your family history, can be daunting. However, by utilising some of the methods outlined in this Chapter, you will find the pursuit of your own family history enjoyable, satisfying and very illuminating.

There are many varied sources of relevant data which are available for research. Some are free, some demand a subscription, while others require the purchase of credits. Libraries, national and local archives are generally free, as are museums and other public facilities. Sometimes the use of a private researcher might be necessary; the fees for this would be subject to negotiation. In addition there are many magazines and numerous reference books devoted to the subject of ancestors and family history. The internet is particularly useful nowadays.

Before embarking on a search of any documentation, the best initial entry to your family history is your own family. Elderly relatives, who might need convincing of your motives, will be a mine of fascinating information. They will have old photographs and other documents which will provide hard evidence to support oral statements. From the start you must keep a record of your conversations as it is so easy to forget details of dates, names and places. Beware that some family secrets might prove embarrassing to your relatives and these must be treated with sensitivity. Every family has matters that are best kept under wraps. Nothing is to be gained by disclosure as valuable information for your research could be withheld if individuals are not confident of your discretion. Talk to as many relatives as possible about your family history project. You will be surprised at the amount of intriguing and valuable data they can give you which you may never have heard about before.

An early twentieth century picture. Fortunately every individual is identified as their names are written on the reverse of the photograph. The place is the Bowling Club, Arbroath, Scotland.

Frensham Hill Staff c. 1905

Staff of the Frensham Hill Estate, Frensham. Surrey. This picture shows the estate's cricket team in 1905. The individuals are not identified.

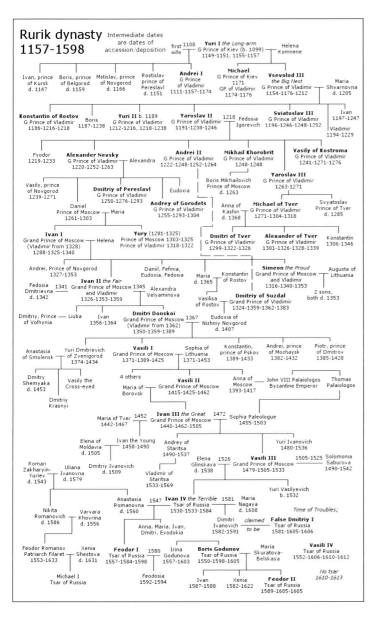

The Rurik family tree.

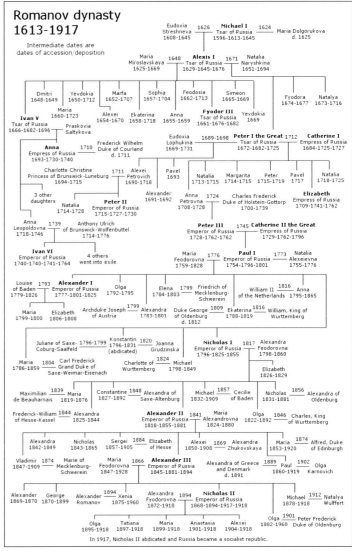

The Romonov family tree.

These documents show the birth and death certificates of Agnes Bone. It can be surmised that her death was due to the influenza epidemic at the end of the Great War.

The obvious relatives with whom to begin your family history research are your mother and father. Record their birth dates, place of birth and occupations; places of work are also important as this can help to locate your parents at any given time. When and where they married, together with your mother's maiden name, are equally important. Information about their parents and grand-parents should be obtained.

Some individuals may not have been raised by their biological parents. They may have been brought up by relatives, friends or have been adopted. In the UK formal adoption did not occur until 1927. Prior to this many simply had informal agreements with relations or friends that they bring up their child. It is common for those who have been adopted to have taken their new parents' surname and they may be totally unaware of the names of their biological parents. This can make it difficult to establish an individual's origins, but careful and sensitive enquiry can often overcome this problem.

Copies of birth and marriage certificates can be easily acquired and cost a modest amount. Older relatives may appear on a published census. The most recent published censuses are 1911 in the UK and 1920 in the USA.

Information on parents is definitely the key which will open doors to all your further research. An additional valuable source of data is family photographs. Ask your relatives to help you to name the individuals, date the event and locate the occasion depicted in the picture. Make a note of this information. It is best to copy a photograph and write relevant details on the back. If you have to write on an original photograph a special pencil

No.	Name and Surname.	When and Where Born.	Sex.	Name, Surname, & Rank or Profession of Father. Name, and Maiden Surname of Mother. Date and Place of Marriage.	Signature and Qualification of Informant, and Residence, if out of the House in which the Birth occurred.	When and Where Registered, and Signature of Registrar.
13	Isabella Steven Findlay	1893 April Ninth 9h. 30m. A.M. Marchburn	F.	James Findlay Railway Pointsman Sarah Rankin Findlay M.S. Houston 1888 October 5th Kirkconnel	James Findlay Father (Present)	1893 April 20th At Kirkconnel William Kirkland Registrar.
14	John C Cowan	1893 May 7 Fourth 11h. 0m. A.M. Kirkconnel Village	M.	William Cowan Coal Miner Janet Pearson Cowan M.S. Jackson 1888 December 4th Kirkconnel	William Cowan Father (Present)	1893 May 13th At Kirkconnel William Kirkland Registrar.
15	Agnes Bone	1893 May Fifth 6h. 0m. A.M. Kirkconnel Village	F.	Samuel Bone Coal Miner Jane Bone M.S. Love 1884 December 26th Kirkconnel	Samuel Bone Father (Present)	1893 May 20th At Kirkconnel William Kirkland Registrar.

can be purchased which will not damage the picture. It is surprising how easily information can be forgotten if it is not recorded immediately.

It is important to remember that memories can be unreliable particularly with the very old. However, as you talk to more and more people you will be able to cross reference the information they give you in order to corroborate any particular data. However, to some extent, all memories are subjective and are reproduced through the perspective, beliefs and views of the individual recounting the story.

The best advice is to treasure your relatives. Get started on recording their memories of events and other relations as soon as possible. Do not forget that memories fade and unfortunately our nearest and dearest do not stay with us for ever – so don't delay and get started today!

CHAPTER 2: RELATIVES

A typical wedding photo is a great reminder for distant relatives.

Her majesty Queen Elizabeth II with Prince Phillip and four of their grandchildren.

The Bush family (top) and the Kennedy family (left) two of the worlds most powerful political families.

The family of Loiuis XIV of France.

CHAPTER 3: PERSONAL RECOLLECTIONS AND MEMORABILIA

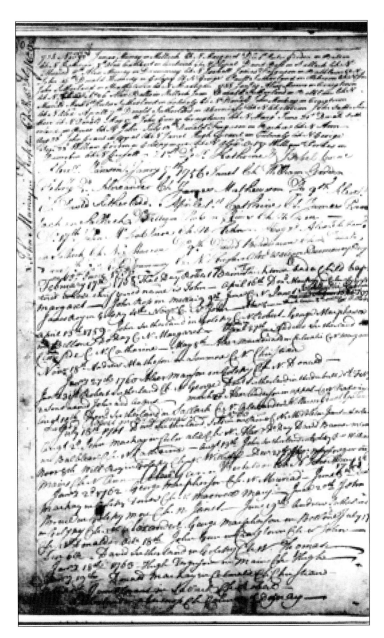

A birth registration page from a church register in Golspie, Scotland 1761. This demonstrates that the writing in these church registers is often illegible

The preferred way to obtain personal recollections is by conducting interviews. It is important to record what you are told during any interview. Consider using a tape recorder or similar device as such equipment provides a very reliable record.

Before you start any interview you should prepare a list of topics about which you wish to ask questions. This is essential because informants are often reticent and will only open up when prompted by specific questions. You should reassure your informant about your method of record keeping as recording equipment or making written notes while interviewing can divert attention away from the subject under discussion. Also reassure interviewees about confidentiality, so that they are willing to disclose all information they may have.

As the interview progresses, comment on how interesting and useful the information is. This will motivate your informants, stimulate interest in your project and encourage them to provide as much information as possible. At the end of the discussion thank the informant and ask whether you can return to them if you need to pose supplementary questions.

Informants will often have various items of memorabilia to back up their statements. For example, they may have photographs of relatives or of events to which they refer. Alternatively they may show you letters written by or to family members. Items such as driving licences, telegrams, vaccination certificates, school reports and certificates or newspaper cuttings may have been kept because they refer directly to an ancestor. Those who have been in the armed forces may have left various documents relating to their service. All such items contribute towards painting a picture, not only of particular individuals, but also of the social context of their lives.

After obtaining both oral accounts and memorabilia from several different family members, try to analyse the

This small folding card dates from the end of the 19th century. It was sent by Lizzie Gibb to her brother Jim. This is a clear illustration of how taste and fashion in such cards has changed. It also demonstrates a stereotypical image of men's difficulties in carrying out minor domestic tasks.

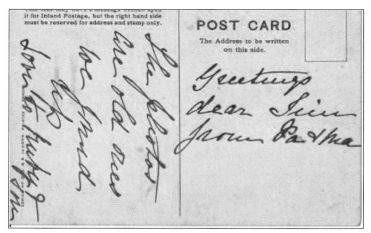

The front cover and reverse of a birthday card sent to James (Jim) Gibb from his mother and father c. 1900.

data you have acquired. Cross reference the information in order to assess whether certain statements corroborate data given by others, or whether memorabilia provides hard evidence to back up oral information. In this way a coherent picture will start to emerge of your family history. At the same time gaps will become apparent in your knowledge. Any such gaps will indicate where you need to go, or what further questions you need to pose, in order to fill in these gaps. In other words, this automatically presents you with your next logical steps in your search for your own family history.

It should also be remembered that from the beginning of the 19th century to the middle of the 20th century there were enormous movements of populations. The Highland Clearances in Scotland caused large numbers of displaced people to emigrate particularly to Canada, Australia and New Zealand. Records exist of many of these, but they are in many different locations. Family history societies in the north of Scotland are the best place to start. Many of the present residents of the Highlands are in a position to offer advice on the likely locations of these natives of Scotland.

The Irish famine of the mid 19th century left many destitute and starving. Large numbers emigrated to England and Scotland, but the greater numbers went to the USA. Records of Irish populations are more difficult to acquire as these were destroyed in 1916, when the Dublin Post Office was set on fire during the Easter Rising. However, relevant Irish websites are referred to at the end of the book.

The largest movement of people in the 20th century stemmed from the persecution of the Jewish people of Europe by the Nazis between 1934 and 1945. Although

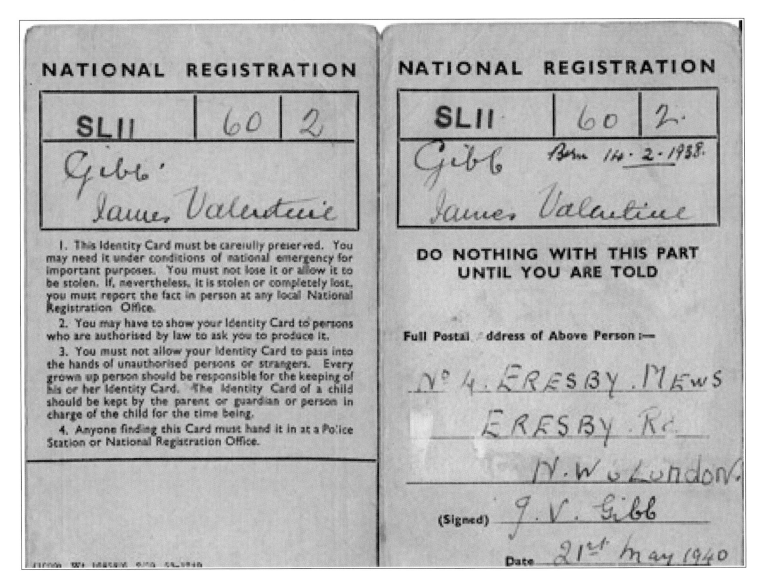

Identity Card issued in 1940

the forced relocation of the Jews was a precursor to their murder in concentration camps, some survived and emigrated, mainly to Israel. Some Jewish people did escape from the clutches of the Nazis prior to the Second World War, with a number of children being sent to safe havens by the Kindertransport organisation.

The Nazis had hoped that the records of these atrocities would be destroyed by the end of the war, but the Allies on both war fronts were able to save many of these and they are now available from various sources. The central database of these is the Yad Vashem, Jerusalem Holocaust Martyrs' and Heroes' Remembrance Authority. Websites for these records are shown at the end of the book.

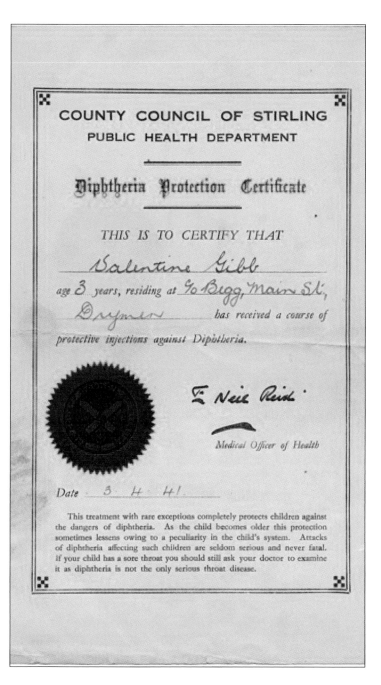

COUNTY COUNCIL OF STIRLING
PUBLIC HEALTH DEPARTMENT

Diphtheria Protection Certificate

THIS IS TO CERTIFY THAT

Valentine Gibb

age 3 years, residing at C/o Bigg, Main St,
Drymen has received a course of
protective injections against Diphtheria.

E Neil Reid

Medical Officer of Health

Date 3. 4. 41.

This treatment with rare exceptions completely protects children against
the dangers of diphtheria. As the child becomes older this protection
sometimes lessens owing to a peculiarity in the child's system. Attacks
of diphtheria affecting such children are seldom serious and never fatal.
if your child has a sore throat you should still ask your doctor to examine
it as diphtheria is not the only serious throat disease.

Vaccination Certificate issued during WW 2

My Dearest Daddy I wish you a happy birthday from your loving little Son Alfred XXX XXX XXX

Birthday Greetings from a son, aged four, to his father, 1907. The tone of this short letter is somewhat different from what one would anticipate a small boy to write to his father nowadays

19

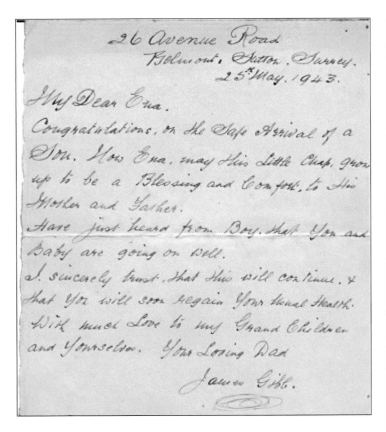

This letter corroborates the birth of a the writer's grandson in 1943.

A Cunard White Star luggage label from the post Second World war era. Prior to the mass use of aircraft in the 1960s, most travel was by sea or train.

A poem sent to Ruby Ethel Gibb by a relative.

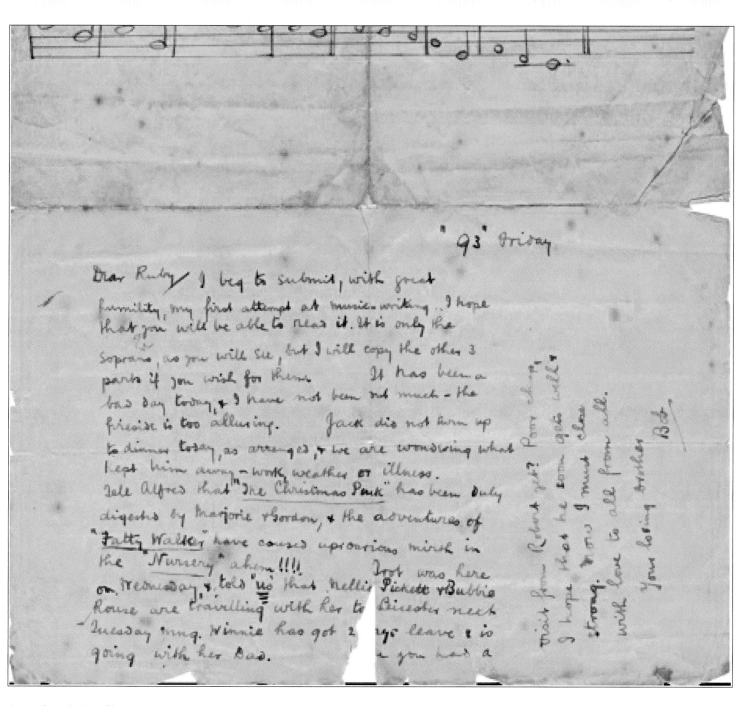

Letter from Robert Gibb to his sister-in-law Ruby Ethel Gibb in 1914.

The above documents show the outer cover and inside details of a timetable for a shipping company operating between London and Dundee in 1914. This was probably a cheaper mode of transport than the railway but took much longer.

Valentine card from James Gibb to Ruby Annett

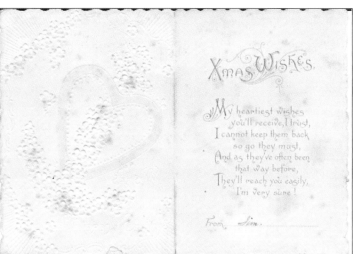

Xmas Wishes

My heartiest wishes
you'll receive, I trust,
I cannot keep them back
so go they must,
And as they've often been
that way before,
They'll reach you easily,
I'm very sure!

From Jim.

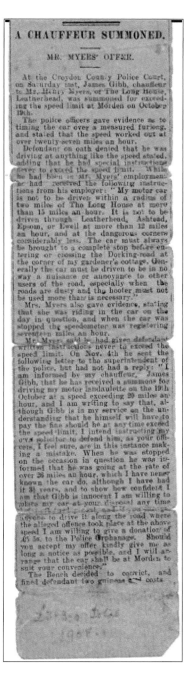

A CHAUFFEUR SUMMONED.

MR. MYERS' OFFER.

At the Croydon County Police Court, on Saturday last, James Gibb, chauffeur to Mr. Henry Myers, of The Long House, Leatherhead, was summoned for exceeding the speed limit at Morden on October 19th.

The police officers gave evidence as to timing the car over a measured furlong, and stated that the speed worked out at over twenty-seven miles an hour.

Defendant on oath denied that he was driving at anything like the speed stated, adding that he had special instructions never to exceed the speed limit. While he had been in Mr. Myers' employment he had received the following instructions from his employer: "My motor car is not to be driven within a radius of two miles of The Long House at more than 15 miles an hour. It is not to be driven through Leatherhead, Ashtead, Epsom, or Ewell at more than 12 miles an hour, and at the dangerous corners considerably less. The car must always be brought to a complete stop before entering or crossing the Dorking-road at the corner of my gardener's cottage. Generally the car must be driven to be in no way a nuisance or annoyance to other users of the road, especially when the roads are dusty and the hooter must not be used more than is necessary."

Mrs. Myers also gave evidence, stating that she was riding in the car on the day in question, and when the car was stopped the speedometer was registering seventeen miles an hour.

Mr. Myers said he had given defendant written instructions never to exceed the speed limit. On Nov. 4th he sent the following letter to the superintendent of the police, but had not had a reply: "I am informed by my chauffeur, James Gibb, that he has received a summons for driving my motor landaulette on the 19th October at a speed exceeding 20 miles an hour, and I am writing to say that, although Gibb is in my service on the understanding that he himself will have to pay the fine should he at any time exceed the speed limit, I intend instructing my own solicitor to defend him, as your officers, I feel sure, are in this instance making a mistake. When he was stopped on the occasion in question he was informed that he was going at the rate of over 26 miles an hour, which I have never known the car do, although I have had it 3 years, and to show how confident I am that Gibb is innocent I am willing to place my car at your disposal any time ... to drive it along the road where the alleged offence took place at the above speed I am willing to give a donation of £5 5s. to the Police Orphanage. Should you accept my offer kindly give me as long a notice as possible, and I will arrange that the car shall be at Morden to suit your convenience."

The Bench decided to convict, and fined defendant two guineas and costs.

Press cutting from Surrey Comet in October 1908

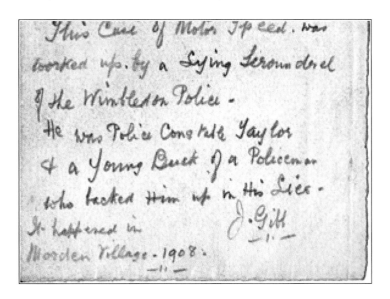

The preceding press cutting shows that James Gibb was fined for speeding in Morden Village, Surrey. His comments on this conviction are recorded in his own hand above. He claims that it was a "fit up". He was fined two Guineas and costs.

Hand made Christmas Card 1903

The inside of the above card, sent from John (Jack) Gibb to Alfred Gibb when he was one month old. John Gibb was a Linotype Operator on the news paper the London Daily Chronicle.

A Christmas Card from John Gibb to his brother Jim satirising the recent birth of his son Alfred.

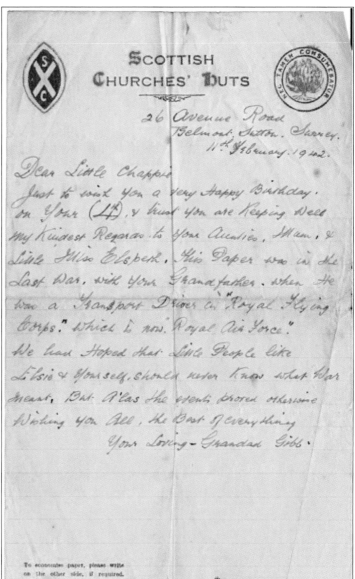

Letter sent to a grandson from loving grandfather during second World War.

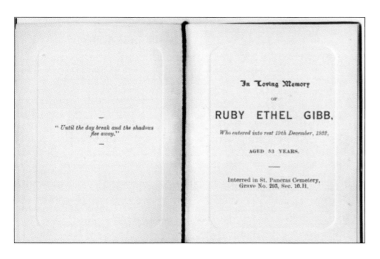

Memorial Card for Ruby Ethel Gibb. It was common at this time to send such cards. Like many other customs it has now gone out of fashion.

A typical birthday card of the 1940s.

Another example of a 1940s birthday card. Note the different use of the word 'gay' in comparison with its contemporary usage.

A civil war medal awarded to a Mr Henry F. Keiser

LAARAKKERS

Fitzhugh

A collection of family crests or caoats of arms.

Simpson

CHAPTER 4: CENSUSES

Census records are a good source of family information. However, it should be remembered that they are only a snapshot of a household which is taken every ten years. In the UK, until the 1911 census, all records were transcriptions of the head of the household's census return. Many mistakes were made by census enumerators when they transcribed the originals. This means that even data acquired from a census could be incorrect.

The oldest extant census is from the Han dynasty in China in 2AD, while the first US census, mandated by the Constitution, was in 1790. It was conducted by US Marshals who went from door to door to record the name of the head of the household and the number of people therein. Slaves were enumerated but only three out of five were counted for apportionment. Native Americans (Indians) were not counted.

The first UK census which is of any use to family historians was conducted in 1841. There had been previous censuses in 1801, 1811, 1821, 1831, but these were limited to furnishing information on men suitable for fighting in the Napoleonic wars. Information on any individual's age, place of birth and occupation only occurred from 1851.

The first systematic count in Europe was taken in Prussia in 1719, but it was not until 1895 that a large-scale census was undertaken in the German Empire.

Unfortunately, while most countries have conducted censuses at regular intervals over the last 150 years, some have deliberately destroyed the returns after obtaining the statistical information. Alternative sources are available such as Post Office directories, voters' rolls, school records and church registers.

A map produced from the Han Dynasty.

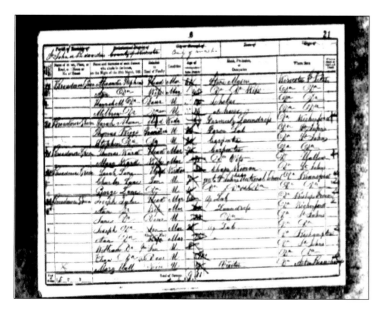

The census of 1851 is the first to be generally regarded as a modern census. It contains ages, place of birth, relationship of each individual to the head of household and occupation. The information is reasonably accurate in-so-far as it was given to the enumerator. However, places of birth could vary, as there were local differences in how a hamlet, parish, village or town were described.

It should also be borne in mind that at this time most people were illiterate and might not have known how to spell their own name. This can lead to anomalies when comparing this data with that contained in later censuses. Furthermore, enumerators tended to spell names the way they were pronounced. This clearly lead to errors and great variations in the spelling of any particular name.

Here is another page of a census. This one dates from 1861. This will allow the researcher to compare data given in censuses from different dates. It would be interesting to compare this with both the preceding census as well as that which follows and dates from 1871.

(Left) This is a page from the 1841 census. This is particularly relevant as it was the first census to have information which is useful to the family historian. It contains names and ages, although the ages may be rounded up or down for juveniles. However it does not give their place of birth but only whether they were born in the county where the census is taking place. It sometimes provides details of occupation. It does not inform the relationship of each individual listed to the head of the household. This information was only provided in future censuses.

Census of 1871

CHAPTER 4: CENSUSES

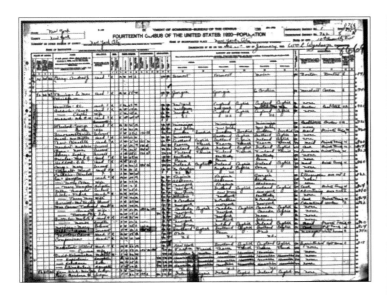

Census New York USA 1920. This American census of 1920 contains much more information than its British counterpart. For example, it includes information regarding the places of birth of both the entrant's mother and father. The number of people recorded on each sheet is greater in its British counterpart. However, it will be noted that the print is much smaller which makes it somewhat difficult to read. The advantage is that entries are not crossed out as is often the case in British censuses. A magnifying glass is very useful when wishing to decipher the contents. On a technical note, the problem of analysing the census information from earlier US censuses quickly and accurately led to the invention of the punched card by Hollerith, who was in fact the Director of the census.

Census of 1851, 1861, and 1871 Scotland. The above documents provide examples of the Census taken in Scotland. They are basically the same as the census conducted in England.

The exterior of the US Census Bureau Building, located in Suitland, Maryland

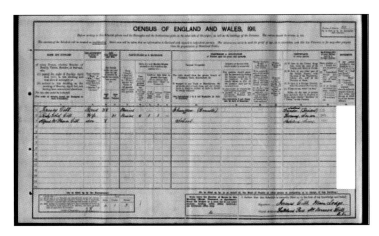

The above document provides a further example of the 1911 Census England & Wales

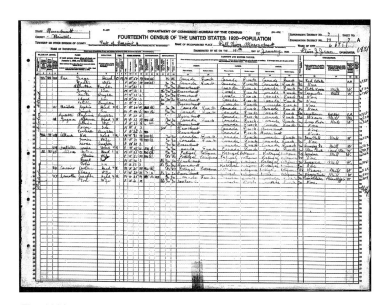

The 1920 census.

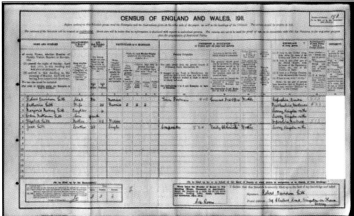

The 1911 census was the last to be published in England and Wales. It will be noted that there are blank columns on the extreme right. These columns contain information about the entrant's mental state. However, it has been deemed approriate to withhold such data until 2011. This particular census was the first to be published in the householder's own handwriting. It also contains additional information regarding the wife's children, both dead and living.

The seal of the US Census Bureau.

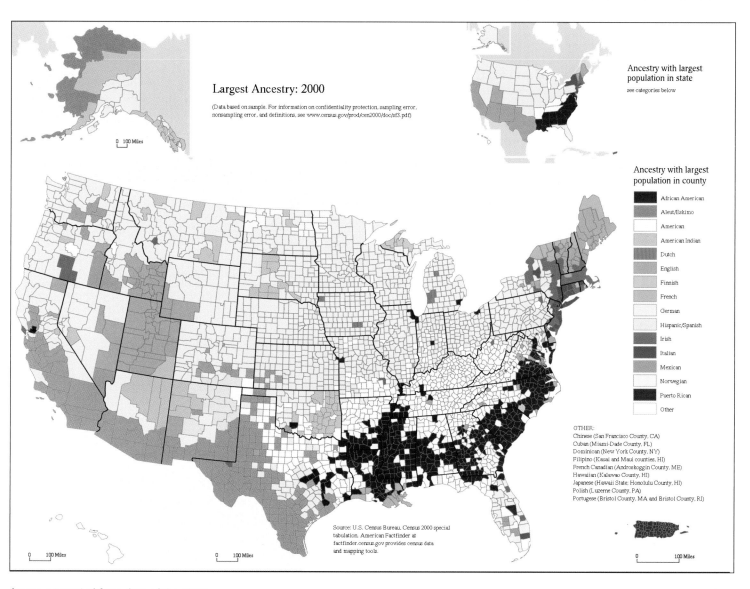

Largest Ancestry: 2000

(Data based on sample. For information on confidentiality protection, sampling error, nonsampling error, and definitions, see www.census.gov/prod/cen2000/doc/sf3.pdf)

Ancestry with largest population in state
see categories below

Ancestry with largest population in county

- African American
- Aleut/Eskimo
- American
- American Indian
- Dutch
- English
- Finnish
- French
- German
- Hispanic/Spanish
- Irish
- Italian
- Mexican
- Norwegian
- Puerto Rican
- Other

OTHER:
Chinese (San Francisco County, CA)
Cuban (Miami-Dade County, FL)
Dominican (New York County, NY)
Filipino (Kauai and Maui counties, HI)
French Canadian (Androskoggin County, ME)
Hawaiian (Kalawao County, HI)
Japanese (Hawaii State; Honolulu County, HI)
Polish (Luzerne County, PA)
Portugese (Bristol County, MA and Bristol County, RI)

Source: U.S. Census Bureau, Census 2000 special tabulation. American Factfinder at factfinder.census.gov provides census data and mapping tools.

0   100 Miles

Image generated from data of the 2000 census.

CHAPTER 5: BIRTH, MARRIAGE AND DEATH CERTIFICATES

In England Birth, Marriage and Death registration became compulsory in 1837. In Scotland, it was not obligatory until 1855. Prior to state registration, churches were the main repositories of this information, but did not in the main record deaths.

Copies of certificates can normally be obtained for a fee from the appropriate registration authority in each country, but recent records might be unobtainable as there are restrictions on who should receive them. One may have to prove that the individual was a close relative and that there is a legitimate purpose to obtaining the record.

The information contained in these records can be of immense value to the family historian, with details such as dates, places and relationships contained therein. But a note of caution, as the information given to the registrar of the event was not normally confirmed by anyone other than the informant, errors can be made, either by accident or design. Death certificates particularly are prone to error, as the informant may not have been familiar with the deceased's family background. Birth certificates can also be suspect if the individual was born illegitimate and a fictional father's name is registered. It is interesting that Church records are usually more accurate than official records, as the minister or priest would be familiar with the family and it is unlikely they would make errors.

Pursuing spurious records can be time-consuming and lead to insurmountable brickwalls. If your research seems to be going nowhere on the basis of what seems to be rock-solid evidence, a little lateral thinking may be in order. Consider looking at other records which are contemporaneous with your record. This will generally present clues and answers to your problem.

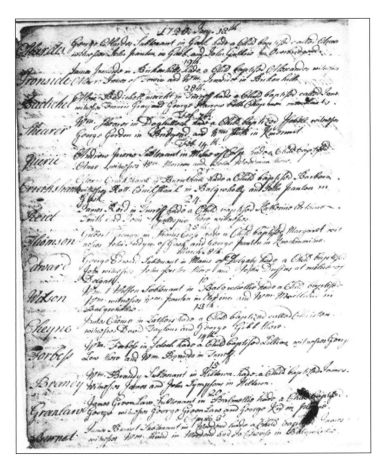

An early birth registration of Katherine Reid in 1720. These parish registers recorded the baptism of a child, rather than its date of birth, but baptism usually occurred within a very short time of birth.

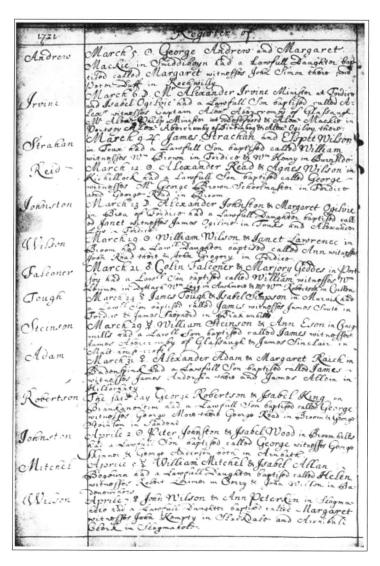

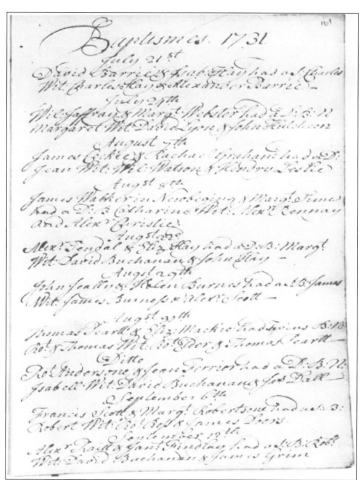

This is a record of the baptism of James Adam in 1721. In this instance the minister who recorded the event also put the child's astrological birth sign against his name. This is an apparently strange practice for a Presbyterian minister.

The above document records the baptism of Robert Rait in 1731. It should be compared with the following document recording the baptism of his daughter, Isabel. It will be of interest if the researcher can note any significant variations between these two baptism records.

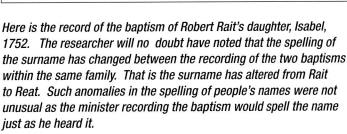

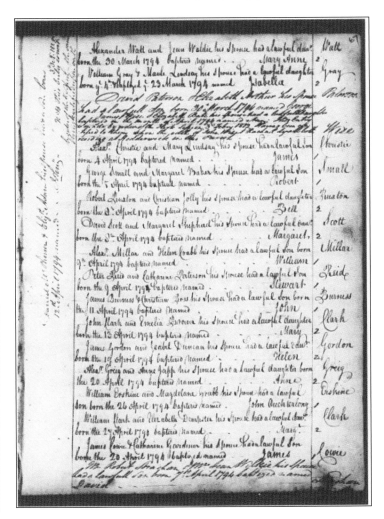

Here is the record of the baptism of Robert Rait's daughter, Isabel, 1752. The researcher will no doubt have noted that the spelling of the surname has changed between the recording of the two baptisms within the same family. That is the surname has altered from Rait to Reat. Such anomalies in the spelling of people's names were not unusual as the minister recording the baptism would spell the name just as he heard it.

Here there is yet another example of a baptism register. In this instance it is in respect of John MacPherson in 1794. At the top left-hand side of the document, written at right-angles, is an instruction from the Kirk Sessions that the MacPherson children should be baptised.

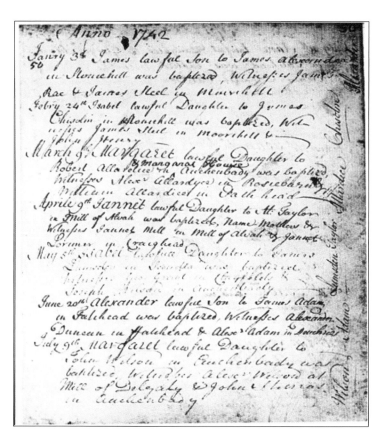

The above document concerns the baptism of Alexander Adam in 1742. It provides an excellent example of the poor handwriting of many ministers of the Church. Contrary to current opinion, the handwriting of many ministers left a great deal to be desired, which represents a recurrent problem for the family historian who researches through ancient documents.

Here is a further instance of the illegibility of many documents. It frequently takes the researcher many hours of patient interpretation to decipher relevant information. In this case, if studied carefully, it will be revealed that Donald McPherson's birth is inserted along with his sister's baptism. Her registration is in 1762, while his birth is in 1761. It is hardly noticeable, but if the researcher uses a magnifying glass and careful interpretation, this information is at the very end of the line. In fact, if the above sheet is examined even more carefully, it will be noted that this birth is recorded yet again at the bottom of the above document.

Letitia Gibb, born in 1869, has been recorded on the document above. However, it is unusual that she went through the procedure of having her name changed within a month. A correction is issued on the document to the right renaming her as Jane Ann. See the note at the left hand side of her birth entry in the copy of her birth certificate above. Such changes of names can lead to problems and confusions for the family history researcher.

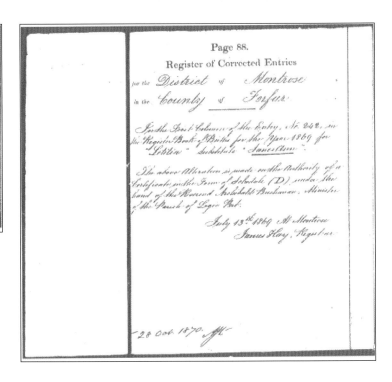

As discussed earlier, the corrected entry for Letitia, now known as Jane Ann Gibb, is documented above. It would be fascinating to know whether it was the father or the mother who got the initial record wrong. Or perhaps a family argument transpired about the naming of the child after she had been registered.

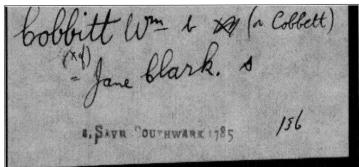

A birth registration from 1857 for Hedley Harry Annett. This is an example of a modern English birth registration. Copies can be obtained at a small fee from the General Register Office.

An example of a church wedding registration in St Saviours, Southwark London in 1785. Note that Cobbitt has an alternative spelling shown in brackets at the end of the line. As he is unable to write, William Cobbitt has signed the register with an 'X'.

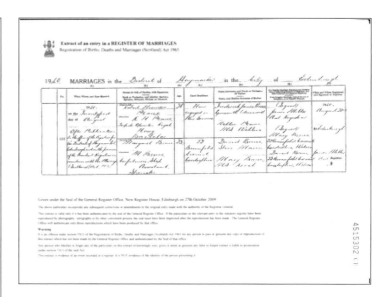

A modern Marriage Certificate relating to Robert N Pearce and Margaret Bruce in 1940. Such certificates provide the researcher with an array of relevant information on occupations, ages and residence.

Death certificate for James Annett 1873 Hampton, Middlesex. Some researchers may find it useful to find the cause of death which is recorded on this certificate. However the terminology used to attribute the cause of death may be outdated. In such instances reference will need to be made to a Medical Dictionary or Medical Listing to ascertain the equivalent modern terminology.

This is a marriage proclamation in respect of Donald Mc Pherson and Elizabeth Adam in 1782. Note that Donald was a corporal in the Sutherland Fencibles, billeted in Montrose at this time. Later documentation reveals that he changed his name to Daniel. This reinforces the notion that it was more common to change names in this era than it is nowadays.

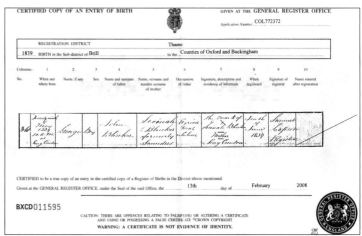

The birth certificate of George Blinker from 1839. Note that this is a reissue of the original.

Copy of a modern death certificate in respect of Lizzie Gibb 1897, Brompton, South Kensington.

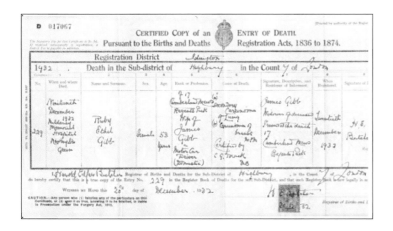

An original death certificate, denoted by the postage stamp beneath the registrar's signature, for Ruby Ethel Gibb 1932 Highbury, London.

A Russian birth certificate

CERTIFIED COPY OF AN ENTRY OF MARRIAGE
GIVEN AT THE GENERAL REGISTER OFFICE

Application Number 121376-3

1861. Marriage solemnized at *Long Crendon Baptist Chapel* in the District of *Thame* in the County of *Oxford and Buckingham*

No.	When Married.	Name and Surname.	Age.	Condition.	Rank or Profession.	Residence at the time of Marriage.	Father's Name and Surname.	Rank or Profession of Father.
38	Eighteenth June 1861	George Blinco	21	Bachelor	Labourer	Long Crendon	John Blinco	Labourer
		Susan Hinton	21	Spinster	"	Long Crendon	Emanuel Hinton	Labourer

Married in the *Baptist Chapel Long Crendon* according to the Rites and Ceremonies of the *Baptist Body*, by me, *William Brown, Minister*

This Marriage was solemnized between us,
George Blinco
Susan Hinton

in the Presence of us,
Emanuel Harris
Jane Shrimpton

John Dudley, Registrar

CERTIFIED to be a true copy of an entry in the certified copy of a register of Marriages in the Registration District of **Thame**
Given at the GENERAL REGISTER OFFICE, under the Seal of the said Office, the **20th** day of **April** **2008**

MXD 753584

The marriage and death certificate of George Blinco. Both are reissues.

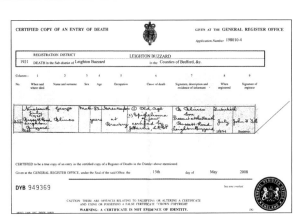

CHAPTER 6: PARISH REGISTERS AND WILLS

A page from a parish register of mid sixteenth century.

Early records can be difficult to read as both the script as well as the language can be arcane. Earlier records may even be written in Latin. Web-sites are available to assist in translating these early documents. This means that the opportunity to obtain information is there although it may take a little time and patience to decipher it.

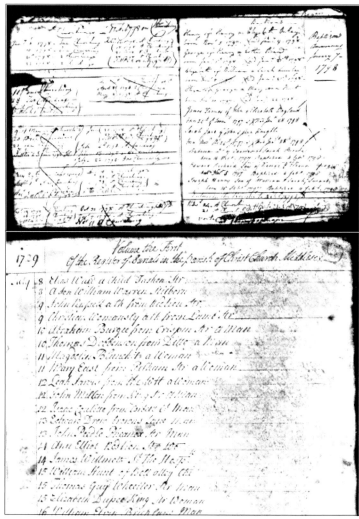

A page from a parish register of the eighteenth century.

Parish registers pre-date most other records. However they usually contain limited information such as baptisms and marriages.

Early wills were recorded by ecclesiastical courts and tend to be dispersed depending on the diocese in which they were recorded. Scottish wills are indexed on the Scotlands People site.

Many more parish records are currently being put online as volunteers digitize the registers. Recently a large number of records pertaining to London parishes were put on-line. Scotland has had its parish records on line for some time and these can be viewed on the Scotlands People site. Most sites require a small fee for downloading a document, although usually the indexes can be viewed for free.

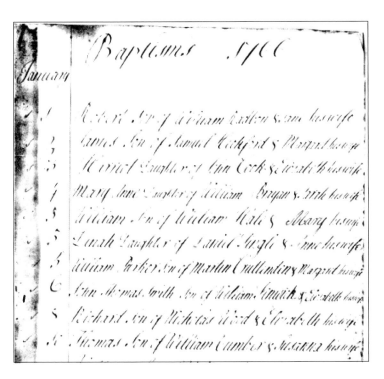

A record of baptisms, date unknown

The front page of an index to wills in Northampton and Rutland on Ancestry.

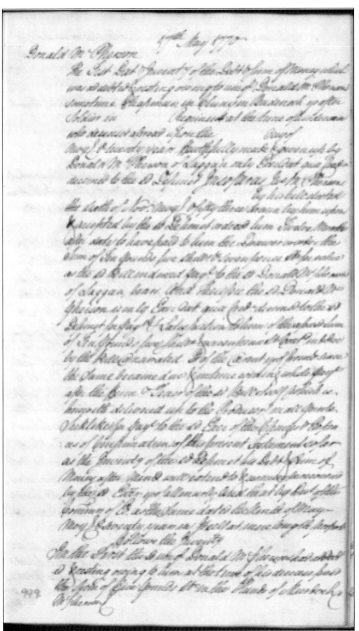

Donald McPherson's will of 1770. The script is easy to read, although the language may be difficult to interpret. These documents would have been written by professional scribes and in many instances their names would be included in the document.

Daniel McPherson's inventory and will of 1839, the year he died. It is twenty pages long and contains all his assets, but not the property he farmed as he was a tenant farmer. He did own some other property which is stated in the inventory. The will is invaluable as it mentions all his children and the proportion of the estate they should each receive after his widow received her legacy. This type of document is of great use because it gives a complete picture of family and business relationships which can be very difficult to ascertain after long passages of time.

John McPherson's will of 1882. Surprisingly, it being a more recent document than the other two examples the writing seems more difficult to read. Until the general use of typewriters all documents would have been written by clerks whose sole purpose would be to carry out such tasks as writing wills.

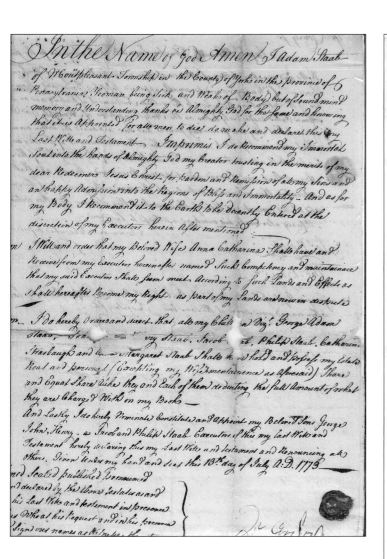

This is the will of Adam Staub

GIVEN this day under my hand and at my dictation the last will and testament of ERNEST LALOR MALLEY lately of Petersham in the State of New South Wales:

I HEREBY give and bequeath all my worldly goods including books and writing implements and mechanical repair tools of trade and watchmaking tools of trade such as remain unto MOLLY RILEY lately of Little Burke Street Melbourne in the State of VICTORIA

And to my only living relative my dear sister ETHEL WINIFRED MALLEY all literary goods and estate being the residue in my literary writings of whatever worth and also unto her heirs and assigns as they may be in future years GOD help us all in those future times
And to the Director of the Maritime Steamship Company, Item: one tusk, Item: two tusks, SIR: I wish to ask if I still owe anything to your account. I wish to change today from this steamship line which I do not even know the name of, in any case, let it be the Aphinar Line.
All these lines are everywhere, and I, powerless, unhappy, can find nothing... the first dog you meet in the street will be able to confirm that. So send me the list of fares from Sydney to Suez.
I am completely paralysed; therefore I wish to be embarked early. Tell me at what time I must be carried on board. HERE ends

Given under the hand of:

Ernest Lalor MALLEY. Signed: ....

Witness: Nurse Doreen ANDERSON. Signed: ....

Dated this ....THURSDaY twenty-second.......... day of ....JULY..........

in the year of our Lord Nnineteen Hundred and Forty-three.

This is an example of a will from New South Wales Australia. It has been taken down in a hospital and dates in 1943.

This is the last Will and Testament of me James Read of No 32 Wyndham Street Marylebone in the County of Middlesex Gentleman In the first place I desire to be buried in my private grave in the burial ground of the Church of Saint Johns Wood Marylebone and in the next place I desire that my just debts funeral and testamentary expenses be paid and satisfied as soon as can be after my decease I give and bequeath all my household goods furniture plate china and other effects except the watch here-after mentioned which shall be in or about my house at the time of my decease unto my grandson James Read absolutely I give and bequeath my small silver watch unto Thomas Bartlett the [illegible] residing near Drury Lane I give and bequeath unto each of my Grandchildren (namely) to the said James Read and to Lucy Read William Read Fanny Read and Henry Read the sum of ten pounds and I give devise and bequeath all that my copyhold house ground and premises called South End House situate in Pond Street Hampstead in the County of Middlesex and also all that my leasehold house situate and being No 30 Sherborne Street Blandford Square in the said County and also all other my real and personal estate to which I am entitled at the time of my decease except what I have disposed of by this my Will or shall do by any Codicil hereto unto my illegitimate son James Read of 14 Wyndham Street aforesaid carpenter To hold the same to him his heirs executors administrators and assigns absolutely And I appoint him sole Executor of this my Will And hereby revoking all former and other Wills and testamentary dispositions by me at any time heretofore made I declare this alone to be my last Will and Testament In witness whereof I have to this my last Will set my hand this twenty sixth day of May one thousand eight hundred and fifty four — James Read — Signed by the said James Read as and for his last Will and Testament in the presence of us both present at the same time who in his presence at his request and in the presence of each other have subscribed our names as witnesses — Fra.s Robinson 48 Conduit Street Hanover Square — James Cordery of the same place his Clerk —

Proved [illegible]

An example of a will from 1858

The will of Robert Jennings. A good example of a hand written original.

A good example of an old parish registry. Dating back to 1822.

CHAPTER 7: MEMORIAL INSCRIPTIONS

Granite tombstone of Josiah Leavitt (1679-1708), Hingham Center Cemetary, Hingham, Plymouth County Massachusetts.

Memorial inscriptions are probably the least used of all family records. In spite of this such inscriptions can contain valuable information and their value should not be ignored. The data included in these inscriptions are invariably accurate as the information is normally provided by close relatives. Unfortunately as time goes by the stones themselves become weathered and worn and thus rather difficult to read.

Fortunately many memorial stones have had their inscriptions recorded prior to their deterioration. These records have been published either in book form or on web-sites. They can be accessed at reasonable cost and are a worthwhile expenditure as they often afford the family historian access to information that cannot be found elsewhere. Relevant sources are given below.

As parish registers generally did not record deaths, memorial inscriptions are sometimes the only records of deaths prior to official registration. The memorial stones can contain much more information than that of the individuals buried beneath. For example, some families who have had loved ones buried elsewhere have the names of the deceased recorded on the memorial they have raised to their late mothers and fathers

Most cities, towns and villages throughout Europe as well as in USA and Commonwealth countries have well-tended war memorials. These relate mainly to the victims of the two World Wars. However, in particular localities they list those who have fallen other conflicts. Many list the names and regiments of those local people who lost their lives in these military actions. The individual headstones in military cemetaries include not only the name and military unit but also age at which the deceased fell.

Elaborately carved grave slab at Shebbear (Devon, England) showing a skull sprouting flowering shoots, as a symbol of resurrection

Captain Andrew Drake (1684-1743) in the Stelton Baptist Church Cemetery in Edison, New Jersey.

Hebrew inscriptions on gravestones in Prague.

Cherished Memories of a
Beloved Husband & Dad

(POP)
Died 31st March 2004
Aged 40 Years
"Missed more than words can say"

Headstone, Haycombe Cemetery, Bath, England

Gravestone showing death date of 1639, Wormshill.

Author Laurie Lee's headstone in Slad, Gloucestershire

Unconventional tombstone in the Cemetery Park of the "Freireligiöse Gemeinde" in Berlin, Prenzlauer Berg. Tree stump headstones in U.S. cemeteries are often associated with fraternal organization Woodmen of the World.

CHAPTER 7: MEMORIAL INSCRIPTIONS

The grave of an infant called Benjamin - Horton graveyard, Northamptonshire

The grave marker for Horatio Nelson Ball and his father, Joseph Ball, Jr. (as well as several other family members) in the Grandville Cemetery, MI. Joseph, Jr. was the son of a Revolutionary War drummer.

Frank Meisler's Kindertransport memorial stands outside Liverpool Street Station.

THIS CROSS WAS ERECTED BY THE PEOPLE OF THIS PARISH IN MEMORY OF HVGH STEWART McCORQVODALE LIEVTENANT THORNEYCROFT'S MOVNTED INFANTRY YOVNGEST SON OF GEORGE McCORQVODALE OF GADLYS WHO AT THE CALL OF DVTY VOLVNTEERED FOR ACTIVE SERVICE IN SOVTH AFRICA AND FELL GALLANTLY FIGHTING ON SPION KOP NATAL ON 24 JANVARY 1900 AND WAS BVRIED ON THE FIELD OF BATTLE.

A memorial for a soldier in Wales, UK.

An example of a tomb, dating back to 1855.

A memorial plaque.

The Vietnam War Memorial in Washington DC.

CHAPTER 8: DIRECTORIES

A 1943 French Street Directory.

A great variety of different directories is published. These directories are catalogues dealing with various categories of information, including specific trades, telephone numbers and addresses, and business locations. We all frequently refer to such directories in our daily lives. However, historic versions are often available which supply basic information to the family historian.

Directories are targeted at specific groups of people. For instance, if your predecessors were engaged in trade there is a very strong possibility that their services would be offered in one of the many directories that were published.

Some directories are indexed on web-sites, but many local libraries permit access to older directories, such as the London Metropolitain Library for London directories. The University of Leicester has a Historical Directories site which contains a wealth of information. Telephone directories have been indexed and can be accessed on-line, a fee is usually charged.

If your ancestor was a minister of religion, Crockfords is a publication for the listing of Anglican vicars and this is widely available. As can be seen from some of the examples on the following page, directories have been published for several hundred years. It is clear that directories are both numerous and varied in content.

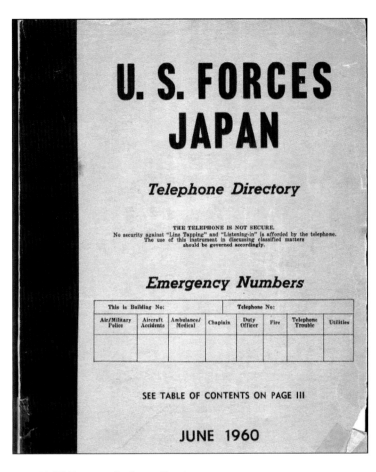

U. S. FORCES JAPAN

Telephone Directory

THE TELEPHONE IS NOT SECURE.
No security against "Line Tapping" and "Listening-in" is afforded by the telephone. The use of this instrument in discussing classified matters should be governed accordingly.

Emergency Numbers

This is Building No:				Telephone No:			
Air/Military Police	Aircraft Accidents	Ambulance/ Medical	Chaplain	Duty Officer	Fire	Telephone Trouble	Utilities

SEE TABLE OF CONTENTS ON PAGE III

JUNE 1960

A 1960 US Forces telephone directory.

The Yellow pages

KELLY'S
DIRECTORY
OF
CAMBRIDGE
1957
(Fifth Edition)

THE BOOK COMPRISES :—
STREETS SECTION
COMMERCIAL SECTION
PRIVATE RESIDENTS SECTION
TRADES SECTION
OFFICIAL INFORMATION; and a
STREET PLAN

KELLY'S DIRECTORIES LTD.
ESTABLISHED 1799
THE OLDEST AND LARGEST DIRECTORY
PUBLISHERS IN THE WORLD
186 STRAND, LONDON, W.C.2
Telephone: Temple Bar 3464 (9 lines)

Price: Twenty Shillings net
© Copyright, Kelly's Directories Ltd., 1957

A 1957 Directory.

A 1905 telephone directory.

A 1922 Telephone directory.

Henderson's

Alberta

Gazetteer and Directory

1914

INCLUDING A CLASSIFIED BUSINESS DIRECTORY OF ALL
BUSINESSES AND PROFESSIONS APPEARING IN
ALL TOWNS AND PLACES THROUGHOUT
THE WORK

PRICE $10.00

COMPILED AND PUBLISHED BY

Henderson Directories Alberta Ltd.

Calgary, Alberta

Copyright, Canada, 1914, by Henderson Directories Alberta, Limited

9

A 1914 Business Directory.

THE TREE TRACERS

Fall
Winter
Spring
Summer

Volume 5
Number 3

Ardmore Notebook 1894

1980-1

1901

SOUTHWEST OKLAHOMA

GENEALOGICAL SOCIETY, INC.
P.O. BOX 5044
LAWTON, OKLAHOMA 73504

Spring
1981

An 1894 geneology directory.

CHAPTER 9: PHOTOGRAPHS

A photograph of William Begg, his wife Jessie and daughter Wilhelmina. It was taken in 1911 at a house called Finich Malis, Drymen, Stirlingshire, where he was head gardener.

All families, however poor they may have been, can bring out of the cupboard their album of the old family photographs. Indeed, photographs of family and friends can be the most exciting, and most readily accessible, records you can obtain. The older the pictures, the more information they can provide which was not possibly available to the researcher from other sources.

Photographs can be particularly informative if the people, dates and places depicted in the photographs are identified. If no dates appear on the picture they can be reasonably established by the identification of the fashion of the clothing. This is especially the case for women, although men's clothing is not such a drastic follower of fashion.

Wedding pictures are very useful in providing a contemporary record of complete families. They contain not only the bride and bridegroom but also their respective parents and other close family members and friends.

Military photographs are informative as they can show regimental badges and rank. The uniform can date a picture as there were frequent changes to style during the 19th and 20th centuries. Books on military dress through the ages are readily available. The plates of different military uniforms can be compared with family photographs to establish the era in which the individual was in military service. These photographs can also indicate a theatre of military activity, particularly with group pictures.

Factory, shop or other commercial organisations had formal pictures taken either in their premises or on leisure outings. These can identify the nature of your relatives' profession and place of work as well as help to fill in gaps in your family history.

School pictures although a recent fashion (the last hundred years) can contain a wealth of information as they almost always have a date and place on them.

VE day party in Gibbon Rd Kingston Upon Thames. You will note the almost total absence of adult males. The only male is the vicar who is located in the middle of the photograph.

A family group taken during the first World War. They are George Foster, his wife Amelia, son John and baby Violet. He is in the uniform of the Vetinary Corps. Note that the son John is in fact clothed in a dress, as was customary at that period.

A street party to celebrate the end of the Second World War. It was taken in Chessington, Surrey in 1945.

CHAPTER 9: PHOTOGRAPHS

A section from a 1961 photograph of pupils at Sleaford Secondary Modern School.

A picture, taken about 1897, of Jack, Lizzie and James Gibb. It was probably taken at Kingston, Surrey. This style of photograph is an Ambrotype, which had gone out of fashion well before this time. The image is a negative on glass which has a backing added to it to create a positive image.

The wedding of Ruby Ethel and James Gibb on 2nd April 1902. Nearly all the individuals in the picture can be identified. The location of the photograph is Kingston, Surrey.

CHAPTER 9: PHOTOGRAPHS

The coachman in the landau is the bridegroom in the previous wedding picture and the location is The Longhouse, Leatherhead, Surrey England.

Alfred Gibb on a horse about 1906, at the Longhouse, Leatherhead, Surrey.

A school photograph of Alfred Gibb who is the son of the couple in the wedding picture. It was taken in Ashstead Surrey in 1907. He is standing in the front row at the left.

A picture taken during the first World War. Alfred is in his scout uniform, James is in the uniform of the Royal Flying Corps, later to be renamed the Royal Air Force. Ruby, although not in uniform, later enlisted in the Womans Royal Airforce.

A family group taken at Ramsgate in Kent in 1926. All the people in the picture can be identified except for the little boy on the left who is not part of the family.

A school photograph taken in 1929. The school is in Edmonton, North London. The pupil marked in the picture by a cross is Catherine Webb, she was thirteen years of age.

An example of a working class school photograph. The children and the location of the school are unknown, but it is probably in Islington, London. This is probably the first time any of these children had their photograph taken. It was taken around the turn of the 20th century.

A school photograph of 1929. One of the children is George Foster, he is marked by a cross. The picture was of a school in Islington, London.

Richmond Road girls school about 1890. Ruby Ethel Annett is on the extreme right of the picture.

A picture taken in 1947 at Drymen School, Stirlingshire, Scotland. The children are dressed for a Christmas party.

Drymen School, Stirlingshire in 1948, many of the children from the previous picture are in this one.

A picture of Valerie Gibb nee Foster at Tiffin Girls School in 1958. The girls are wearing dresses they had made themselves. Valerie is on the left of the photograph.

CHAPTER 9: PHOTOGRAPHS

School photos are a good resource for information. This is a section from one taken in 1961.

Another school photo taken in 1930.

Microsoft Corporation executives (L-R)Chairman Bill Gates, Chief Research and Strategy Officer Craig Mundie, Chief Software Architect Ray Ozzie and Chief Executive Officer Steve Ballmer gather, June 14, 2006, in Redmond, Washington, prior to the announcement of Gates' two-year transition to Chairman and the expansion of Ozzie's and Mundie's responsibilities.

CHAPTER 9: PHOTOGRAPHS

A photo from 1926 showing the employees of Standard Oil.

A handily captioned photo from 1909 of a French family.

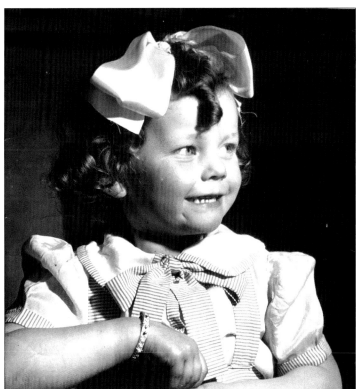

Childhood pictures of the author and his wife in the 1940s.

CHAPTER 9: PHOTOGRAPHS

A series of photos showing two generations of the publishers family. The children below are the son and daughter of the child second from the left in the main photo.

A typical wedding photo. This one showing the groom, his bride and his younger brother.

CHAPTER 10: MILITARY RECORDS AND DOCUMENTS

Ruby Ethel Gibb
WRAF 1918
No. 2 Stores Depot Regents Park
RAF

A photograph taken in 1918 of a Royal Airforce Stores Depot at Regents Park, London. The main body of personnel are Women's Royal Airforce members. They were demobilised at the end of the the First World War

Every family will have had at least one member who had military connections. This will mainly be male relatives. However, it should be remembered that many females served in WW2. Some women were in newly formed military units in the first world war, but these were in vastly smaller numbers than women in the Second World War.

Military records, perhaps surprisingly, are very comprehensive.They go back in some instances several hundred years. Most of these muster lists tend to concentrate on officers, but there are records of soldiers and sailors serving during the 18th century in the National Archives at Kew. Records exist of all the sailors who took part in the battle of Trafalgar. There is a web-site address devoted to this. A high proportion- about sixty per-cent of the WW1 army records were destroyed by bombing in WW2, although some of the " burnt records" as they are called can still be accessed on pay-per-view sites. RFC/RAF officer records from WW1 are available, but not other ranks at present. These, together with Royal Navy records, are available in the National Archives. A fee is charged for the record but not the index.

Ruby Ethel Gibb in the driving seat of an RAF stores depot truck. Her husband who had been invalided from the RAF is shown standing beside her.

The most complete records of deaths, caused by war, is the Commonwealth War Graves Commission. These records also contain details of civilian deaths. This site is free and not only records the date of death, but the location of a grave if one exists. It should be remembered that many, many casualties have no known grave and their memory is recorded on war memorials near their place of death. Some of the records contain details of their next of kin if known. There are other lists of casualties from WW1, but they are not as complete as the CWGC records. It should be borne in mind that your relative may have enlisted under a false name. This may not have been for malign motives, but they may have been under-age when enlisting and feared being found out if they used their real name.

Many people with similar names appear on military records. Therefore it is of assistance if one can provide some details of the regiment or corps, squadron, name of ship/s, in which your relative served. A service number is very useful although these could change, especially if the individual transferred from one service to another.

Medal lists are accessible on the National Archives and can be downloaded for a fee.

John (Jack) Gibb shown front left. He was a Sapper in the Royal Engineers. He is shown here at a camp in Weybourne, Norfolk before going to France. He was killed in April 1918.

Spr. John Gibb, R.E., No. 554432.

Killed in Action on 17th April, 1918.

"And say to all the world 'This was a man.'"
—Shakespeare

Out in the bleak deserted fields of France,
Where once Mars' sword caused ghoulish fiends to dance
    And life's-blood run:
There stands a cross of wood—rough hewn—unstained
A symbol of Eternal Life attained
    By God's own Son.

When called upon to take part in the strife,
He emulated Christ—he gave his life
    And crossed the span.
His memory shall live with us for aye,
And from our hearts, in years to come, we'll say:
    "This was a man."

—W. Douglas Gibb.
1920.

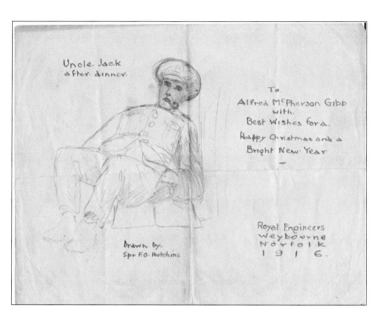

A Christmas card sent to Alfred Gibb by his uncle John (Jack) Gibb Christmas 1916. The picture is drawn by a fellow Sapper F.O. Hutchins.

Alfred Gibb in Scout uniform during the First World War. Scouts played a significant part in carrying out volunteer duties at this time. Alfred Gibb was sent to a camp where the boys harvested flax, which was used in the manufacture of fabric for fighter aircraft.

Gordon Gibb, Alfred Gibb's cousin, who being younger in age was a Cub Scout at the end of the war.

Sunday 14

Dear Uncle John
          I hope that you are still in the best of health. I have started at the Paddington Technical Institute and I like it very much. We learn others things beside Engineering such as Physics. Chemistry and Mathematics. To-day we have had our troop flag presented to us by Lord Claud Hamilton and we are now the proud (posses) possessors of it. The Lord made a speach to us about scouting and about looking after our colours. I expect you remember Mr Grey-breeks at Reece-mews will he has join the Army and is in France Mother wonders if you would

care for the Observer each week as she would post it on to you
          I remain
          Your Affec
          Alfred

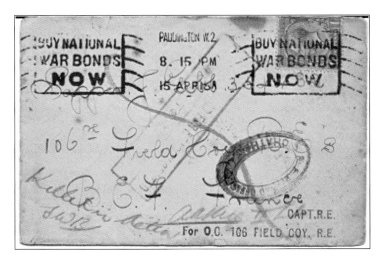

A letter sent by Alfred Gibb to his uncle John Gibb in April 1918. As can be seen from the envelope above, John Gibb was killed in action before he received the letter.

John Elkington , a member of the Machine Gun Corps killed in action in November 1916. He has no known grave and is remembered on the Thiepval Memorial in Northern France.

106 Field Coy R.E.,

B.E.F.

21. 4. 18.

To Mrs J. Gibb,

25 Glenthorne Road,

Kingston-on-Thames.

Dear Madam,

It is with the deepest regret I have to inform you of the death of your husband, Sapper John Gibb.

He had only been with my Section a short time, and yet, by his unassuming manner and great coolness in action, he was soon held in affection by the other Members of our severely tried Section.

Your husband had, with our Company, fought for several days without ceasing.   He fought with bravery and distinction against an enemy greatly superior in numbers.

It will be some consolation to you to know that he greatly helped to stem the enemy flood, fighting, as he did, in the front lines all the time.

It will also perhaps be of some slight comfort for you to know that he was spared the sufferings of the severely wounded, for he was instantly killed, together with another boy of my Section,- whilst getting a brief sleep in a trench - by an enemy shell.

We buried them both where they fell at a point about ¾ mile S.W. of Dranoutre marking the place grave with cards attached to a rifle.   Being in action we could not do more at the time, but should we again visit the place in quieter times, we shall not forget those who served with us so faithfully and well.

I would not attempt to beguile from you, Madam, the

(2)

the great grief which must be yours at the loss of so brave a husband, yet it must be some consolation to know that he did not die in vain, but that, by his sacrifice, England and all that she means to us still lives.

With deepest regrets,

Believe me, Madam, to be,

Yours very sincerely,

(Sd) ARTHUR A RICH IlLt. R.I

(O.C. No. 2 Section 106 Field Coy.)

The letter informing the wife of John Gibb of his death in 1918.

General Sir Ian Hamilton, Commander of the British Forces in the Gallipoli campaign. James Gibb was his chauffeur in the early twenties.

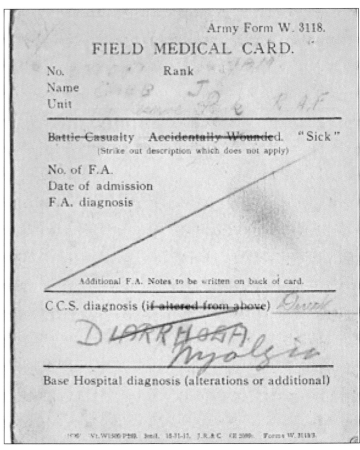

James Gibb's Field Medical Card. He was discharged suffering from dysentery in 1919.

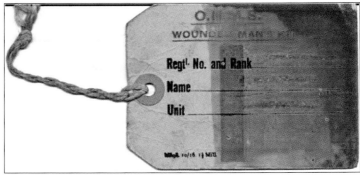

The label which was attached to a wounded man's kitbag.

ROYAL AIR FORCE.

Form 330.

Certificate of Conduct and Ability for Civilian Subordinate.

Date _17/10/19._

UNIT or DEPARTMENT _H. of Stor Dept. Regent Park_

THIS IS TO CERTIFY THAT _F. Little_

served in this {Unit / ~~Department~~} as a _Driver T._

from _March 3rd, 1919_ to _present day_

during which time {his / ~~her~~} conduct has been _exemplary_

and {his / ~~her~~} work _highly satisfactory_

{His / ~~Her~~} age at entry on _____ was shown as

_____ years _____ months, and {he / ~~she~~} has

now been discharged in consequence of _Dept being_

down to day.

This document is not a voucher of identity.

Commanding _Transport Section_

_No. 6_ R.A.F.

A reference certificate for discharged members of the Royal Air Force

The marriage of Robert Norman Pearce to Margaret Bruce in 1940. He was a submariner on HMS Truant at this time. He survived the war.

CHAPTER 10: MILITARY RECORDS AND DOCUMENTS

A group of REME Craftsmen at Hawkins Barracks, Tidworth, in 1959.
They were all National Servicemen.

The Duke of Montrose looks on as Mrs Wilkie places a wreath of
flowers on the war Memorial in Drymen Stirlingshire, Scotland in 1946.
Behind is the Revd. Mentieth. The person holding the banner pole is
Robert (Toby) MacMillan. This war memorial has now been moved to
accommodate a new road.

General Henry Prince of the 2nd Division, 3rd Corps, and Staff - Culpeper, VA.

12th Royal Lancers in India with the Duke of Connaught's Cup 1929.

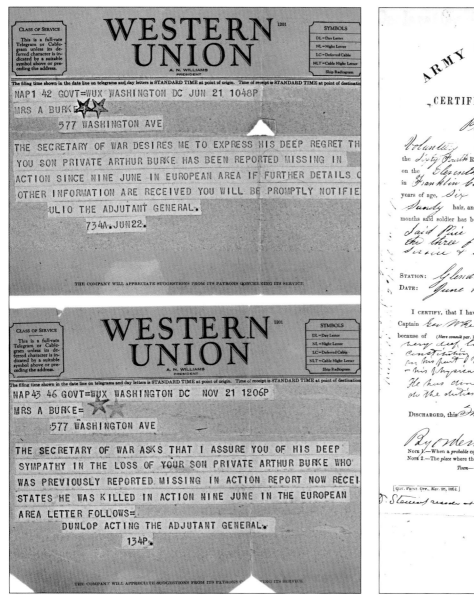

A world war II telegram detailing the death of a soldier.

A certificate for the discharge of a soldier.

Kaiser Karl visits Pergine Airfield in this photo from World War I.

WWI Austro Hungarian Military Band

The Chinese Military Honour Gaurd.

CHAPTER 11: FAMILY LETTERS AND DOCUMENTS

Family letters, birthday cards, Christmas cards and other documents can contain a wealth of information and should be carefully preserved. This does not mean keeping every card that a relative may send you, but storing significant examples, particularly if they contain relevant information about family circumstances to help future generations, who may wish to continue the story of your family, remember to write the names, dates and occasion on the reverse of the documents which you deem worthy keep-sakes.

As with all unique documents these precious mementos should be stored in acid-free plastic pockets and labelled clearly.

Letters naturally will be the most informative of all possible memorabilia. This is because they will usually have the date and the sender's address as well as comments relating to the social context of the correspondence. That is, the contents will hopefully relate family business, which will help to build a picture of your relative's circumstances and lead to a greater understanding of their life.

It is unfortunate that sometimes when someone dies an overzealous relative or friend has a clear-out of all their personal belongings, particularly letters, postcards etc. Treasured memories end up in a dustbin along with a great deal of invaluable family history. This can be a sensitive subject but try to obtain these records by diplomatically suggesting to older members of your family that they may contain valuable information to the family historian and should be preserved. Assurances should be given that any information of a sensitive personal nature will be kept secret until it can no longer embarrass anyone.

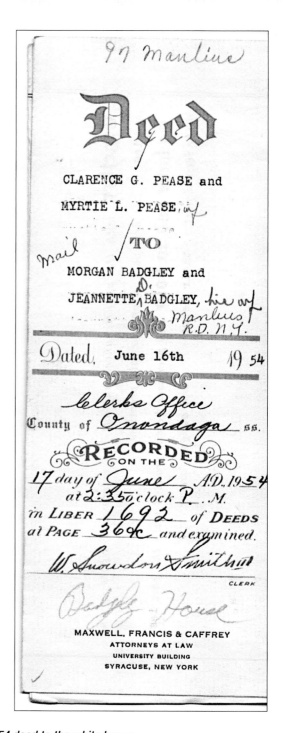

The 1954 deed to the white house.

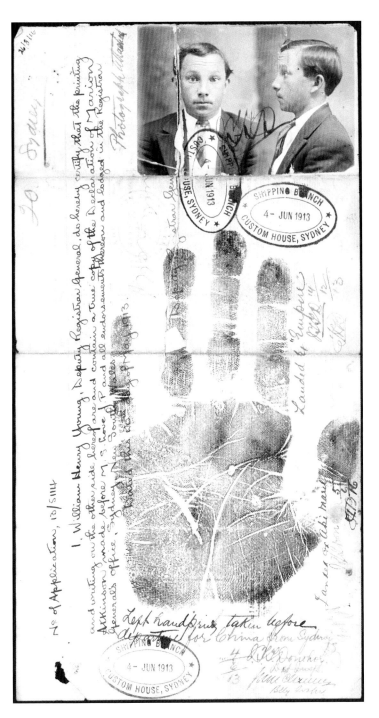

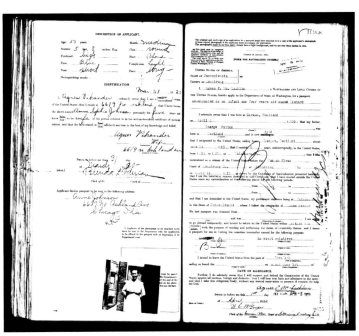

Another example of a vintage passport.

A 1938 British passport.

A vintage passport.

DESCRIPTION OF APPLICANT.

Age: 46 years.   Mouth: moustached

Stature: 5 feet, 8 inches, Eng.   Chin: round

Forehead: normal   Hair: dark

Eyes: blue   Complexion: normal

Nose: straight   Face: oval

Distinguishing marks

IDENTIFICATION.

Feb. 8th , 19 21

I, Camille H. Artru , solemnly swear that I am a {native / naturalized} citizen
of the United States; that I reside at San Francisco, Calif. ; that I have known
the above-named John Gergas personally for 6 years and
know {him / her} to be the identical person referred to in the within-described certificate of naturalization; and that the facts stated in {his / her} affidavit are true to the best of my knowledge and belief.

C. V. Artru

1426 Pacific St., San Francisco, Calif.
(Address of witness.)

Sworn to before me this 8th day   Cashier
of February , 19 21

[SEAL.]

Clerk of the Court at Passport Agent.

Applicant desires passport to be sent to the following address:

614 May St.,
Vallejo,
California.

A duplicate of the photograph to be attached hereto
must be sent to the Department with the application,
to be affixed to the passport with an impression of the
Department's seal.

The application must be in duplicate and accompanied by three unmounted photographs of the applicant, not larger than three by three inches in size, one of which is to be affixed to the passport by the Department; the other two must be attached to this application and its duplicate, respectively. The photographs must be on thin paper and should have a light background. The one not attached to the applications should be signed by the applicant across its face, so as not to obscure the features.

This blank must be completely filled out. The legal fee of one dollar, in currency or postal money order, and the applicant's certificate of naturalization must accompany the application. The same should be carefully read before mailing the application to the Department of State, Bureau of Citizenship, Washington, D. C.

[EDITION OF 1914.]

[FORM FOR NATURALIZED CITIZEN.]

UNITED STATES OF AMERICA

STATE OF California
CITY & COUNTY OF San Francisco } ss:

I, Claes Thorsell , a NATURALIZED AND LOYAL CITIZEN OF THE UNITED STATES, hereby apply to the Department of State, at Washington, for a passport.

I solemnly swear that I was born at Karlskrona, Sweden
on or about the 29th day of September , 1 883 ; that my father,
Peter Thorsell , was born in Sweden
(Country.)
now residing at deceased (1917) ; that I emigrated to the United States, sailing on
board the from Antwerp Belgium
about , 1 903 ; that I resided 18 years, uninterruptedly, in
the United States, from 1 903 to 1 9 at California
that I was naturalized as a citizen of the United States before the Superior Court
of California in and for the City County of San Francisco
on July 20th , 1 910, as shown by the accompanying Certificate of Naturalization;
that I am the IDENTICAL PERSON described in said Certificate; that I am domiciled in the United States,
my permanent residence being at Los Angeles , in the State of Calif. ,
where I follow the occupation of Master Mariner . My last passport was obtained
from none on
(Date.)
and was I am about to go abroad temporarily, and
(Disposition of passport.)
intend to return to the United States within 3 {months} with the purpose of
residing and performing the duties of citizenship therein; and that I desire a passport for use in
visiting the countries hereinafter named for the following purpose:

Sweden   Family Business
(Name of country.)   (Object of visit.)

England   Travel
(Name of country.)   (Object of visit.)

(Name of country.)   (Object of visit.)

I intend to leave the United States from the port of New York
(Port of departure.)
sailing on board the " Drottingholm" on May 2nd , 19 21
(Name of vessel.)   (Date of departure.)

OATH OF ALLEGIANCE.

Further, I do solemnly swear that I will support and defend the Constitution of the United States against all enemies, foreign and domestic; that I will bear true faith and allegiance to the same; and that I take this obligation freely, without any mental reservation or purpose of evasion: So help me God.

Claes Thorsell
(Signature of applicant.)

Sworn to before me this 8th day
of February , 19 21

[SEAL OF COURT.]

Clerk of the Court at Passport Agent.
[OVER.]

A vintage United States passport.

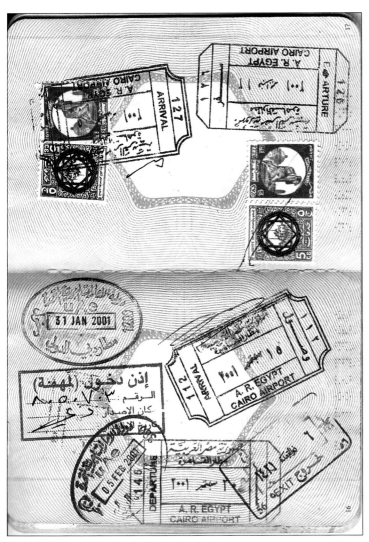

A well travelled modern day passport.

A vintage Parisian passport.

A selection of letters and documents.

SOUTH CAROLINA
STATE HIGHWAY DEPARTMENT
MOTOR VEHICLE DIVISION
COLUMBIA

№ 23129

Received ___ *J. E. Ruppe Gaffney* ___ *12 30* ___ , 192 *7*
of ___ in the amt. of $ *12 55*
(Name)   (Address)   (Cash-Check, etc.)
For the following:
(1) $ *12 55* In payment of 192 *8* License for *Oakland Four*
(2) $ ___ In payment of Bond for transmissal to Magistrate.
Name ___ Address ___ For appearance
in above named Magistrate's Court at ___ o'clock, ___ , 192 ___ for
Trial on charge of violation of the Motor Vehicle Laws of South Carolina.
MOTOR VEHICLE DIVISION,

By ___ *B. G. Spur*
(Inspector District No. ___)

A 1927 South Carolina drivers license.

A letter from Abraham Lincoln dated 1863.

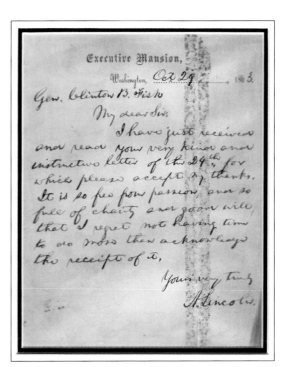

A fairly recent 2005 land deed.

A 1913 share certificate.

A pension record.

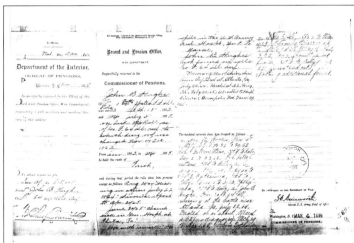

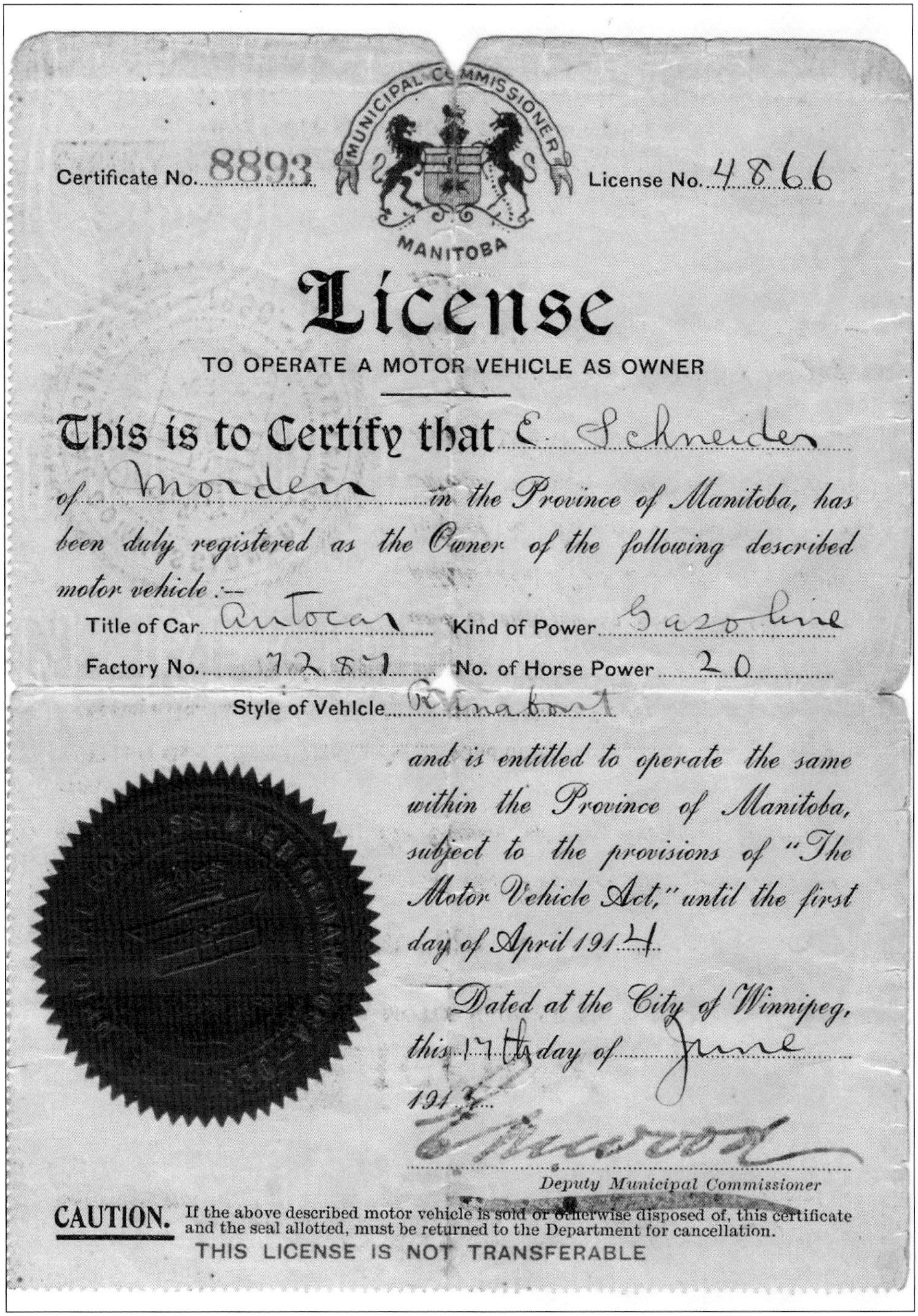

Certificate No. 8893 MUNICIPAL COMMISSIONER MANITOBA License No. 4866

License

TO OPERATE A MOTOR VEHICLE AS OWNER

This is to Certify that E. Schneider of Morden in the Province of Manitoba, has been duly registered as the Owner of the following described motor vehicle :—

Title of Car Autocar Kind of Power Gasoline

Factory No. 7287 No. of Horse Power 20

Style of Vehicle Runabout

and is entitled to operate the same within the Province of Manitoba, subject to the provisions of "The Motor Vehicle Act," until the first day of April 1914.

Dated at the City of Winnipeg, this 17th day of June 1913.

Deputy Municipal Commissioner

CAUTION. If the above described motor vehicle is sold or otherwise disposed of, this certificate and the seal allotted, must be returned to the Department for cancellation.

THIS LICENSE IS NOT TRANSFERABLE

A 1914 drivers license

EXPLANATION OF MARKING SYSTEM

E (Excellent) represents outstanding and superior work.

G (Good) represents work that is above average and shows definite ability in the subject.

S (Satisfactory; passing work) indicates average work; it represents a sound passing grade without tendency toward failure.

P (Poor work but passing) is assigned to those students who have done low, mediocre work, but who still deserve to pass. However, all such grades indicate that the student has barely passed the subject.

F (Failure with condition) indicates that the student has not passed the work. Intensive work may remove the condition.

FF (Final failure) represents that the student is definitely below school standards, that he has done so little work and has made so little effort, he must, consequently, take the course over.

SIGNATURE OF PARENT OR GUARDIAN

First Report *George O Burroughs*

Second Report *George O Burroughs*

Mid-Year Examination *George O Burroughs*

Third Report *George O Burroughs*

Fourth Report *George O Burroughs*

Promoted to Grade *Eight*

Date *June 13, 1952*

Remarks

Merchantville Public School

School Year, 19...—19...

REPORT OF

Burroughs, Frances E

Grade *7*

Teacher *Charity*

Success in school life is, in a large measure, determined by the amount and quality of a student's achievement. Satisfactory achievement, whether measured in quantity or quality, is dependent upon many factors such as ability, ambition, health of the student, home conditions, interest, and, most important of all, the amount of time and effort spent in study.

Most students are quite incapable of preparing all or most of their lessons during their scheduled study periods. A careful survey indicates that the average student should devote from **one and one half to three hours** in home study daily.

Most of our school failures are traced to excessive outside social activities, indifference, lack of home preparation and poor health.

J. EDGAR BISHOP, Supervising Principal.

A example of a report card.

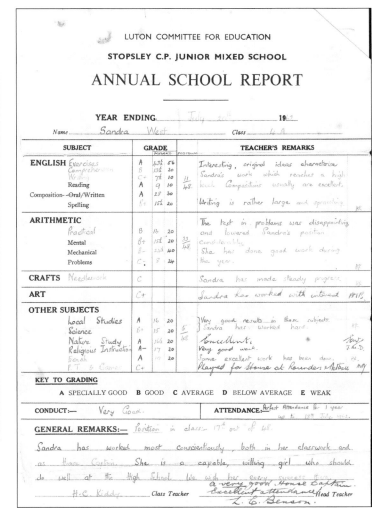

Junior Boys' Dept. Anfield Road C.P. School, Liverpool 4.

Name...Kenneth...Jacob.........Class..4²......Year.2ⁿᵈ.....

Number in Class..42..   Class Teacher's estimate
                          of general Progress
July 1956   during the year.

	Position	Class Position	
English	3	5th.	Kenneth has worked
Arithmetic	13		very well this year

Test Mark or Grading

		as his examination
Art	B	results show. He is
Geography	B	most painstaking and
Handwork	B	careful. His work is
History	B	always neat. In class
Music	B	he is friendly but
Nature Study	B	rather shy.
Physical Education	C	

Grading A - Above class average   Class Teacher M.M.Williams.
         B -   class average   Head Teacher..............
         C - Below class average

Two more report cards.

LUTON COMMITTEE FOR EDUCATION

STOPSLEY C.P. JUNIOR MIXED SCHOOL

ANNUAL SCHOOL REPORT

YEAR ENDING: July 20th 1962

Name: Sandra West   Class: 4A

SUBJECT	GRADE (Marks / Position)	TEACHER'S REMARKS
ENGLISH Exercises	A 43½ 56	Interesting, original ideas characterise
Comprehension	B 13½ 20	Sandra's work which reaches a high
Writing	C+ 7½ 10 11/48	level. Compositions usually are excellent.
Reading	A 9 10	
Composition-Oral/Written	A 28 30	
Spelling	B+ 15½ 20	Writing is rather large and sprawling.
ARITHMETIC		The test in problems was disappointing
Practical	B 14 20	and lowered Sandra's position
Mental	B+ 15½ 20 33/48	considerably.
Mechanical	B- 22½ 40	She has done good work during
Problems	C- 8 24	the year.
CRAFTS Needlework	C	Sandra has made steady progress.
ART	C+	Sandra has worked with interest
OTHER SUBJECTS		
Local Studies	A 16 20	Very good results in these subjects
Science	B+ 15 20 5/48	Sandra has worked hard.
Nature Study	A 16½ 20	Excellent.
Religious Instruction	A- 17 20	Very good work.
French	A 10 20	Some excellent work has been done.
P.T. & Games	C+	Played for House at Rounders, Netball

KEY TO GRADING

A SPECIALLY GOOD   B GOOD   C AVERAGE   D BELOW AVERAGE   E WEAK

CONDUCT:— Very Good.	ATTENDANCE:— Perfect Attendance for 1 year up to 13th July 1962.

GENERAL REMARKS:— Position in class 17th out of 48.

Sandra has worked most conscientiously both in her classwork and as House Captain. She is a capable, willing girl who should do well at the High School. We wish her every success. She is a very good House Captain. Excellent attendance.

H.C. Kirkby   Class Teacher   L.E. Benson. Head Teacher

The Commissioner of Pensions:

    I was the wife of the person on account of whose service during the Civil
War I am drawing pension, during the period of his service in said war, and therefore I request consideration of my case with a view to the allowance of the $50
rate provided by the act of July 3, 1926.

Aug 4   1926.

Name *Louisa E. Bank...*

Address *Bethel Springs*

Tenn

Widow Cert. No. *290.752*

A pension request letter

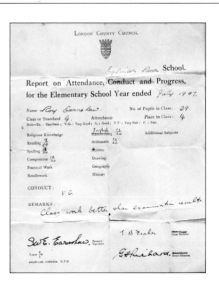

A 1947 school report.

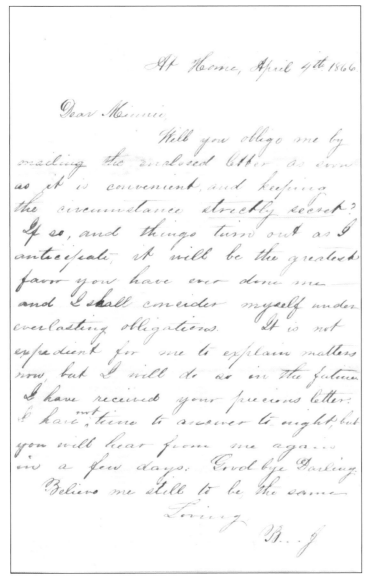

A letter from 1866.

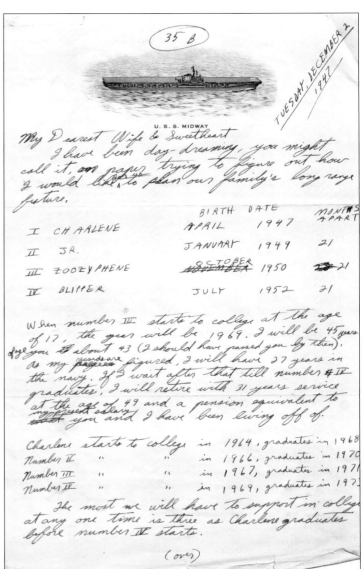

A letter dated 1947.

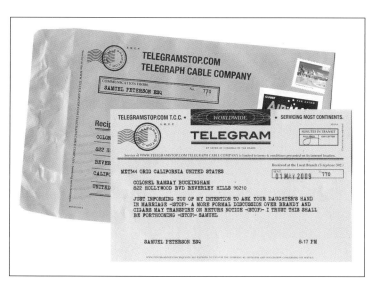

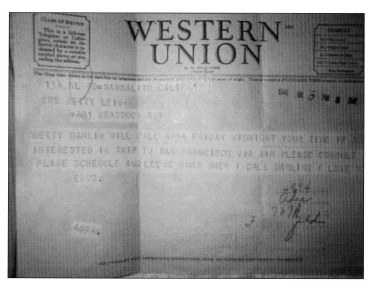

Two examples of telegrams, a modern one and a fairly vintage one.

Dear Honeygirls:

Here we are again! Arrived yesterday about 2:00 and was quite happy to find the weather was considerably cooler than it was on our last trip down. Jerry and I have a room out on Cambridge st., hardly anyone of the recruiting party stayed at the Fresno Hotel as their rooms are 2.00 a night and for 10 days it would really run into money. I don't know what the lady were staying with will charge for the room but it won't be anything like the price of the Fresno.

My cold does'nt seem to get any better but I have hopes that it will soon as Ive had it almost a week now. My money is holding out pretty good, Ive got 10.00 left and payday is Friday. The only thing I will have to do is eat and pay for my room. Jimmy has'nt sent me my raincoat as yet. He has'nt been able to get out of the horspistol. But he will probably send it in the next two weeks.

Will you send me Mel's address I know a chief at Farragust. He's a swell guy about Mel and my age, he's some kind of a Specialist; takes groups of sailors all over the country and kind of does S.P. duty. Johny Hendershot told me that Perry and his wife separated. But we surmised that a year ago. Northridge is sure a changed man he almost bends over backwards to be nice to us. We have it figured that in the old day's when he was so damn mean the cause was over- work and worry which would cause him to be that way. He is still arrogant, tho. Tell me some more about your raise and the reaction of the bigsh?ts. We are going to go into blues when we return to Sacto, thank goodnes. I'm so tired of these whites, they look like the devil after two days and you have to continually be running to the laundry. When I come down I will pick up my other set, also remind me to take that extra tie hm with me I can't use it as its too long and Horner would like to have it.

I took a pair of shoes to have them half soled and boy what service they give the Navy. I could have had them the following day if I wanted to. They only charge 1.50 for half soles. What difference does it make whether Faye works at the place or anywhere else. It only takes her 15 minutes to get there from our house. Incidentally did Mel sell the car, and for how much? It was sure an easy get-off, $200.00 to his former wife, does he have to continue paying now? It looks as if there going to start drafting fathers, which in my estimation and many other peoples is lousey. They will probably draft a few thousand and in 3 or 4 months discarge them all which will of course wreck their lives temporarily: disrupt their home life, and probably cost them their jobs. Did Arsenaur ever get a ruling on his appeal?

The first group of fellows just arrived so will have to close. I sure miss you honeygirls and wish the hell I were back in S.F. with you.

Write to NAVY RECRUITING STATION
FRESNO, CALIF.

Love and kisses,

Claude

A letter sent during World War II.

CHAPTER 12: RECOMMENDED WEBSITES

This is a list of very useful websites. It is not exhaustive, but there is a sufficient variety to cover most families. Cyndislist has the most comprehensive leads to other websites, Ancestry and Find My Past are very good for census and births, marriages and deaths. As you proceed with your searches, you will find as I have done that specific sites give you most of the information you require.

Ultimately you will find that websites are insufficient for your research and that visits to national archives and libraries are necessary. The staff is these establishments are extremely helpful and patient and are very willing to pull out all the stops to assist you.

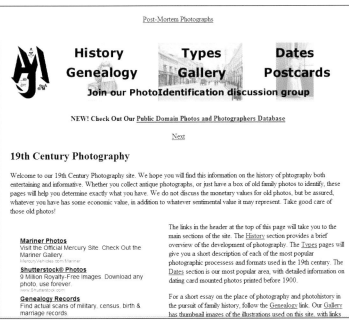

http://ajmorris.com/roots/photo 19th Century Photo Project

www.1911census.co.uk   1911 England & Wales site

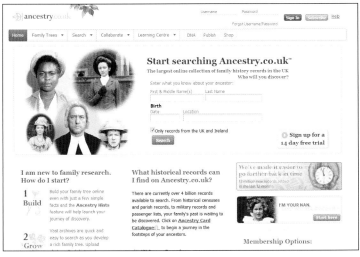

www.ancestry.co.uk General pay site

www.york.ac.uk/inst/bihr Borthwick Institute at York University

www.censusfinder.com Census finder

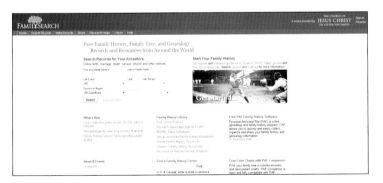

www.familysearch.org The Church of Latter Day Saints (Mormons)

www.cyndislist.com Lists of family history sites

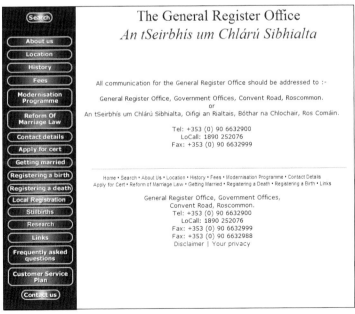

www.groireland.ie Eire records

CHAPTER 12: RECOMMENDED WEBSITES

www.ellisisland.org   US immigration records

www.gro.gov.uk/gro/content/certificates Birth, marriage & death certificates UK

http://wiki.fibis.org   Families in India

www.ffhs.org.uk   Family History Societies

www.freebmd.org.uk   Births, marriages & deaths to 1920

www.genuki.org.uk General site

www.groni.gov.uk Northern Ireland records

www.genesreunited.co.uk Pay per view site

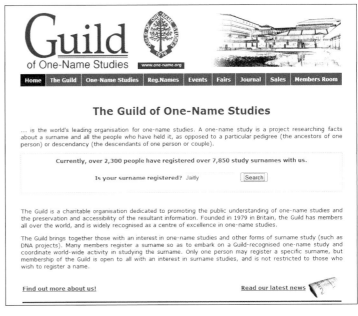

www.one-name.org Guild of One-Name Studies

www.yadvashem.org Central database of Shoah victims

CHAPTER 12: RECOMMENDED WEBSITES

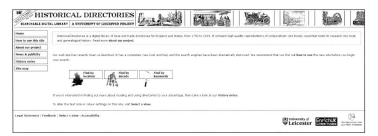

www.historicaldirectories.org   Directories UK

www.irishtimes.com/ancestor Irish records

www.immigrantships.net Records of immigrants

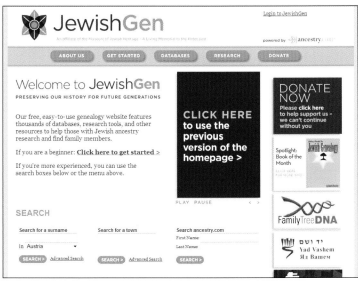

www.jewishgen.org   Jewish records

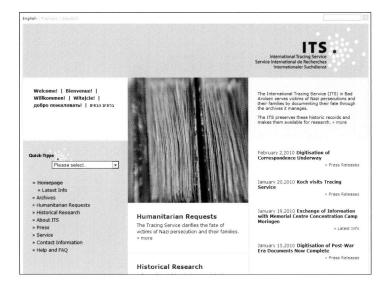

www.its-arolsen.org   Records of prisoners, forced labourers & children

www.cityoflondon.gov.uk/londonGenerations City of London records

www.scotlandspeople.gov.uk Site for all Scottish records

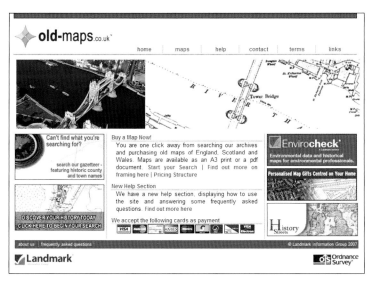

www.old-maps.co.uk Old maps UK

www.genuki.org.uk/Societies General site

CHAPTER 12: RECOMMENDED WEBSITES

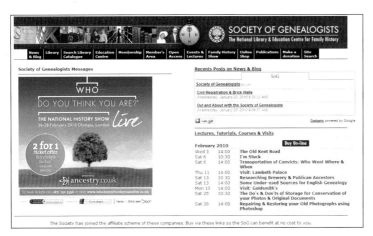

www.sog.org.uk   *Society of Genealogists*

www.1914-1918.net *The Long Long Trail, First World war site*

www.twgpp.org *The War Graves Photo project*

www.workhouses.org.uk   *Workhouses UK*